Brendan McAloon is a reformed journalist and television producer. He established Rip Curl's Search TV series, co-produced Mick Fanning's award-winning biopic surf film *Mick, Myself & Eugene*, and was a television producer for professional surfing's World Championship Tour. He followed his 2009 surf/travel memoir *Deep Water: Travel stories & the search for the perfect wave* by editing  the journals of the original surf explorer Peter Troy (*To the Four Corners of the World*) in 2011. He lives on Victoria's west coast with his wife and two children.

SHARKS NEVER SLEEP

BRENDAN McALOON

hardie grant books

This edition published in 2018 by Hardie Grant Books,
an imprint of Hardie Grant Publishing
First published in 2016

Hardie Grant Books (Melbourne)
Building 1, 658 Church Street
Richmond, Victoria 3121

Hardie Grant Books (London)
5th & 6th Floors
52–54 Southwark Street
London SE1 1UN

hardiegrantbooks.com

A Cataloguing-in-Publication entry is available from the catalogue of the
National Library of Australia at www.nla.gov.au

Sharks Never Sleep
ISBN 978 1 74379 370 1

Cover design by Josh Durham
Cover image courtesy of Universal Images Group, Getty Images
Text design by Patrick Cannon
Typeset in 11.5/16 pt Berkeley Oldstyle by Cannon Typesetting
Printed by McPherson's Printing Group, Maryborough, Victoria

CONTENTS

INTRODUCTION

IT BEGAN WITH surfing. I contracted that life-altering virus on summer holidays in Port Fairy, a pretty fishing port on the southern edge of Australia. I grew up two hours from the nearest beach yet became as addicted as the most strung-out junkie – a landlocked country kid infected with a deep longing for else-where. I gravitated towards the coast before I was old enough to drink beer or drive a car, surviving on Saturday morning bus rides to Barwon Heads and blue heaven Big Ms. Ocean swells are ephemeral, but for the next two decades I arranged my life around the friction of wind on water, chasing the perfect waves of my teenage dreams. For years, leaving the coast was like holding my breath, anxiety bubbling beneath my breast.

Then the anxiety morphed into something else. It began in Western Australia in 2010, when Nick Edwards was mauled to death by a great white shark while surfing at South Point near Margaret River. My eldest son was barely a year old. There were three more fatal shark attacks in Western Australia in 2011. There were another two in 2012. By the time Chris Boyd was killed while surfing at Umbies, just around the corner from South Point, in November 2013, I had a wife and two kids to consider. I couldn't help but think of them at home, asleep in bed, while I paddled out in the muted pre-dawn light, baubles of cray weed casting dark shapes across the ocean floor. There were five fatal shark attacks in Australia in 2014 and a record high of 33 attacks in 2015, including a brutal fatality on the far north coast of New South Wales that sent shockwaves around the country and beyond.

My local beach is normally a quiet, unremarkable stretch of sand between Point Roadknight and Urquhart Bluff on Victoria's Surf Coast, but in January 2017 it was at the epicenter of a rush of shark sightings and beach closures. As a naïve and idealistic young university student, I would inscribe Francis Bacon's famous quote 'Knowledge is power' on the inside cover of my notebooks. The following is my attempt to exorcise the fear with facts: true stories of encounters with sharks, those man-eating monsters of myth.

PART ONE

1

THE LAST RIDE OF
TADASHI NAKAHARA

THE GREAT FISH glided quietly around the outcrop of ancient, barnacle-encrusted rock and tracked back towards the shore, following the coastline south, around the cape. Moving majestically, the fish swept its powerful tail from side to side as it swam along the easternmost edge of Australia, past white-sand beaches and rocky headlands fringed by rolling hills, rainforest and sleepy holiday towns. It was hunting, invisible below the surface, camouflaged from both predator and prey. Beams of morning light penetrated the Pacific, dancing across the dirty-grey dorsal fin, but the enormous shark merged with the darkness of the ocean deep. Seen from below, its white belly blended with the sun-dappled surface.

At Seven Mile Beach, a lone fisherman stood in ankle-deep water, casting into the boat channel. An olive-green bream darted skittishly across the gutter. Neither saw the distinctive conical snout, underslung mouth curved in a permanent sneer and dead black eyes of the most fearsome predator on earth as it cruised silently by, around Shag Rock, past Boulder Beach and Iron Peg, moving mindlessly south like a prehistoric torpedo.

Darren Rogers turned right at the East Ballina Cemetery and wove through the clutter of holiday houses and faded apartment blocks set atop the ridge, gazing towards the horizon. It was one of those sluggish, slow-motion summer mornings. Stale heat rose from the shadows of the mangroves and waterlogged swamp oaks lining the waterways that veined the quiet northern New South Wales town. The sun was hot, piercing the thick blanket of humidity and bouncing off the bitumen of Beach Road as it sloped down past the lighthouse towards the sea.

Darren checked the surf from his usual spot at Ballina Head, with Shelly Beach to the north and Lighthouse Beach to the south, where the Richmond River rock wall pokes out into the Pacific, its basalt blocks spilling down into the water. The ocean was smooth, and orderly lines of swell swept shoreward, cresting and peaking into perfectly formed waves. Beyond the rock shelf at Shelly Beach, two small clumps of surfers floated either side of a deep channel, riding the ebb and flow of the ocean. Darren hadn't surfed for almost six months because of a serious neck injury, but today the urge was irresistible.

Tadashi Nakahara swooped around the base of the wave in one graceful arc, tucking his slender body into a low crouch, left arm extended, as the wave curled over him. Brooke Mason stroked over the shoulder, hooting and hollering, as Tadashi disappeared inside the barrel: a silhouette speeding past, lost in a mist of spray.

Brooke laughed, sat up and adjusted her bikini, unable to wipe the smile from her face. The summer sunshine, tropical water and picture-perfect surf had been a distant dream for the 19-year-old surfer from the southern suburbs of Hobart. But now she was here, having arrived in Byron Bay only the day before to begin a year-long break from studying medicine at the University of Tasmania. Tadashi paddled alongside Brooke, both grinning like a pair of Cheshire cats. There was a lull in the swell and they spent a moment drifting, talking about how good the waves were, how beautiful the day was and Tadashi's young son in Japan.

Meanwhile, Darren Rogers pushed his surfboard through the shallows, navigated a line of broken whitewater and began paddling for the horizon. Out to sea, Tadashi had moved deeper than the other surfers. He straddled his surfboard, toes dangling in the water, and waited.

The great fish sensed vibrations in the water; its electroreceptors detected subtle changes on the surface. It rushed up from the deep, gaping jaws hinged open to 150 degrees, revealing a bloody-pink gum line and jagged, uneven rows of serrated teeth. It hit Tadashi like a bolt of lightning, dragging him underwater.

'I think I would've been about ten to fifteen metres diagonally from Tadashi,' Brooke recalled. 'I watched him move out of the corner of my eye and I looked at him and just saw him take a huge breath and go under. I thought he was just going for a swim. All of a sudden there was a big splash and pretty much instantly, there was just blood everywhere. There was blood right near me – it spread out in the water so fast and there was just so much blood. He got pulled down so deep and his board got pulled down with him. My brain just kind of realised, "That's a shark attack."

'My legs were quivering. I kind of looked away and looked back. There was just blood but he wasn't there. I didn't know where he was. I was split between deciding whether I should paddle further out to him or to paddle in. My fight or flight response took over and I started to paddle in. I was focusing on just one stroke at a time. Pretty much my mind had gone into a kind of war zone mode. I sort of thought that everyone would be attacked – you sort of think you're about to die. All the other guys in the water were paddling in and everyone was quiet and no-one was yelling. There were no waves to come in on. It was the scariest moment of my life.'

Quiet is not Brooke's natural state. The bubbly blonde with cherubic cheeks and a grin as wide as a watermelon slice talks quickly, with sentences chasing each other to fill blank space. Brooke is usually a ball of manic energy that runs on one speed: 'flat knackers'. She surfs with the same joyful zest – fast and loose, with a dynamite forehand snap. She had won the Under-21 division of the Tasmanian leg of the Subway Summer Surf Series a few months before deferring her studies and moving to Byron to chase waves and train at Surfing Australia's High Performance Centre at nearby Casuarina Beach, with hopes of becoming a full-time professional surfer.

Brooke loves surfing almost more than anything.

'I love everything about it,' she said. 'Being out in the water, riding waves, is like nothing else. It's so much fun.'

While her favourite surf spots are wild places, like Cloudy Bay at the southernmost tip of Tasmania's Bruny Island, Brooke has always been 'really terrified of sharks'. She won the ABC's 2012

Heywire story competition with a tale about a trip to Boneyards, a remote Tasmanian surf break, fretting about 'shark-infested waters' and 'preparing for what to do if a great white fancied me for afternoon tea', only to scald her legs with two-minute noodles.

'Danger lurks in the most banal of places,' she concluded.

Ballina's Shelly Beach is not a banal place. On that fateful Monday morning it was Brooke's idea of paradise, with perfect waves and dolphins swimming through the warm, crystal-clear water; everything was bathed in sunshine, light and laughter – a realisation of Tom Blake's 'blessed church of the open sky'. Blake was an American surfing pioneer who 'almost single-handedly transformed surfing from a primitive Polynesian curiosity into a 20th century lifestyle', according to Matt Warshaw's *Encyclopedia of Surfing*. In Blake's 1969 book, *Voice of the Atom,* the surfing guru riffed on the spirituality of riding ocean waves, expressing a philosophy rooted in the intrinsic balance of the natural word, concluding simply that 'Nature = God'.

But by the time Brooke reached the rocky shoreline of Shelly Beach, the natural world had warped into an Old Testament vision of evil and violence. Her paradise was lost; her dream upended.

'I have had nightmares like this,' she confessed. 'It was so prehistoric. No matter how much we like to pretend that humans are in control of our environment and we've made all these advances, it was literally like nature, the predator, in its natural environment and we were so vulnerable and helpless.

'The scariest thing was that there was no warning. I didn't see the shark. I just saw Tadashi go under. I was so shocked and I was still so scared of the shark. Even on the land, I was scared of the shark coming and attacking. I turned around and saw this guy, it might have been two guys, just struggling with this body and I was like: "Oh my god, I've got to do something now." You know, you're split, because you just want to be so brave but you want to stay alive. I think it nearly broke my heart, the bravery of those guys, and it made me think, "I want to be brave too." The bigger guy who was in the water with me, he was like: "Take my board, I'm going to help him in."'

The 'bigger guy' was Darren Rogers. Darren is an imposing figure. He is built like a bouncer, his muscular body etched with tattoos and scars. His head is shaved, and dark orbital rings encircle his intelligent blue eyes. Fifty years old, Darren is a lifelong surfer and committed practitioner of traditional Indonesian martial art, pencak silat. He is a solitary man and a serious, deep thinker. Yet, in the moment that would change his life, he acted on pure instinct. He gave his surfboard to Brooke and re-entered the blood-soaked water.

'Everything happened real fast,' he explained.

Unlike Brooke, Darren hadn't witnessed Tadashi's attack – he had still been paddling through the broken water closer to shore. 'Everyone started coming in. Every surfer knows what that means. So I spun around and came back in too. You usually just wait for a bit, it might be a false alarm, and you go back out. But then I saw two guys out through the channel, quite a distance out, trying to drag something. They were paddling with one arm and going really slow. I thought, "Something is not right." I ripped my leg rope off, ran up onto the rocks and jumped back in. I got out to the channel and that's when I saw him. He was already unconscious and I could see that his legs were gone just below the hips. I just thought: "Fuck."'

Darren realised that they had to act quickly and get Tadashi out of the water. 'When I saw the extent of his injuries I knew almost immediately that it was a great white. Only a very big shark could inflict that level of injury. We were trying to hold his head and body out of the water as best we could, sort of struggling and wading, knowing the entire time that there was a massive shark in the water nearby and knowing that sharks often come back a second time after an attack. Eventually we made it back to the rocks and picked him up, clambered over the rocks and up onto the sand. Everyone was screaming, looking at this guy with his legs bitten off. Everything went into overdrive, like flashes in a film.'

Brooke had taken the leg rope off her surfboard to use as a tourniquet.

'I've done first aid and first year medical school so I wanted to help,' she said. 'He was unconscious and had lost so much blood. He had no legs – there was only about an inch of leg left. For some reason that didn't really freak me out because I'd cut up dead bodies at med school. I wrapped the leg rope around his whole torso to try and stop the blood flow. There was so much teamwork. I just sat and held his head in my hands and said to him, "You're safe and you're okay." I just said anything I could think of to relax him while they started doing CPR.'

Darren kneeled beside Tadashi, leaning over him to perform mouth-to-mouth. He pinched Tadashi's nostrils then placed his mouth tightly over Tadashi's, breathed two quick breaths and leaned closer to listen for breathing and to see if he could feel Tadashi's breath on his cheek. 'I was watching his chest rise and fall as I was breathing into him. The others had lifted his legs to keep the blood flowing to his heart and his head, so I was looking across at his legs. It was really intense and I was completely unprepared. I didn't realise how intimate CPR is. It makes sex look like something that's almost inconsequential, you know what I mean, something that's not even important. In my experience, there's nothing more intense [than performing mouth-to-mouth]. I've had some heavy experiences in my life but this took it all to a new level of intensity … and just horror.'

A crowd of around 30 people had gathered on the beach, surrounding Darren, Brooke and the small group of surfers working furiously to bring Tadashi back to life.

'I could hear sirens in the background and there were people crowding around,' Darren recalled. 'It was very claustrophobic. Then I thought I got a breath – his chest moved and I thought I saw his eyes move. I yelled at everyone to be quiet and I put my ear to his mouth, but I was told later that it was probably just his brain shutting down, sending a few final pulses of movement. I kept doing mouth-to-mouth until the paramedics came. It seemed like forever. I've heard it was between seven and ten minutes, which is quick responding, but it felt like eternity.

As the sirens got closer, Brooke ran up to the car park to guide the paramedics to Tadashi.

'I raced up the hill to the ambulance and [the paramedic] handed me a defibrillator and something else,' she said. 'I went to run back down to the beach and he stopped me and told me to calm down. I thought every second was crucial but the paramedic said to me: "This guy pretty much has no hope of surviving." That was shattering to hear.'

'I looked up at the paramedic's face and I knew that was it, that there was no chance, because he knew what he was looking at,' Darren said. 'I did too but you can't stop. The paramedic said: "Keep going, keep going, you're doing an excellent job." He got his machine out and took some readings and eventually told us to take our hands off and said: "Sorry, but you have to step away." Everyone was screaming. I was still holding his head because you have to tilt the head back when you're performing CPR. I didn't let go of his head until the police told me to.'

'When [the paramedics] went over and pronounced him dead, he was just lying there for ten minutes and there was all these kids around,' Brooke said. 'It was like a horror scene.'

'I got [the police] to put a blanket on him because it was really full on,' Darren said. 'Then I took off. I knew the media would be there real quick. I went down to the showers and I was shaking and I was dry retching. I got out of the shower, got in the car dripping wet, and drove off. I was freaking out.'

'Me, another girl and a few of the paramedics carried the body up,' Brooke said. 'His stumps were rubbing against my arms the whole time.'

Darren does not like to think about it, but is consoled by the belief that Tadashi did not suffer.

'He was unconscious before he was dead,' Darren explained. 'The actual point of death was somewhere within that journey. I was staring into his eyes the whole time and there was a moment there that his eyes changed, they dilated more, but I don't know. It was heavy. He would've lost consciousness within seconds [of being bitten], so in my opinion his last memory would've been of his last wave.'

2

THE GIANT, MAN-EATING SEA MONSTER

AFTER INSPECTING TADASHI'S lifeless body, marine biologists from the NSW Department of Primary Industries (DPI) confirmed that the Japanese surfer had been attacked by a 4-metre great white shark.

The great white (*Carcharodon carcharias*) is a legendary creature – an ancient predator that floats in the deep, dark recesses of beachgoers' imaginations around the world. In 1975, Steven Spielberg turned Peter Benchley's best-selling thriller about an enormous killer shark terrorising the fictional New England town of Amity Island into a summer blockbuster. *Jaws* broke box office records, overtaking *The Godfather* as the highest grossing film of all time, and launched Spielberg's illustrious career. Inspired by a news report about Long Island fisherman Frank Mundus catching a 2-tonne great white with a harpoon in 1964, *Jaws* created a monster scarier than Norman Bates, Jason Voorhees, Chucky and Freddy Krueger combined – for, unlike those flights of fancy, the giant, man-eating sea monster was *real*, lurking beyond the shoreline of a beach near you.

It was easy for Benchley, Spielberg and co. to make the great white shark into such a convincing monster with almost mythic qualities: there was barely any scientific knowledge of this enigmatic creature.

'In those days, it was common knowledge that sharks were not only carnivores, they were omnivores; they would eat anything,' Benchley explained in a 1995 article for *Popular Science* magazine. 'They would attack, kill and devour human beings without much, if any, provocation.'

Such information was based upon assumption, ancient folklore and inventive untruths. Shark stories. They date as far back as 440 BC, when the Greek 'father of history', Herodotus, wrote about 'sea monsters' devouring shipwrecked Persians in the Aegean Sea. An antique vase unearthed on the island of Ischia in the Tyrrhenian Sea adorned with an image of a sailor being attacked by a shark is even older, dated by archaeologists to around 725 BC.

The shark has 'come down through history with a reputation as an ancient, mindless, man-eating, ship-following, eating machine that should by rights be eradicated from the face of the earth', according to American naturalist Richard Ellis, who has written and illustrated numerous books on the subject.

Swedish botanist and zoologist Carolus Linnaeus appended a note to his description of the great white in 1758 suggesting that 'it is likely that the prophet Jonah remained in the belly of this animal for a space of three days [and] three nights'.

The Florida Museum of Natural History in landlocked Gainesville is home to the longest-running database of shark attacks, the International Shark Attack File (ISAF). ISAF's records begin somewhere south of Jonah, in 1580, with an English naval officer's account of the 'terrible death' of a crew member who fell overboard on a journey from Portugal to India. As the sailor was being hauled back to the boat 'there appeared from beneath the surface a big monster known as tiburón', Spanish for shark. 'It rushed at the man and cut him to pieces right before our eyes.'

Duunnn dunnn! Duuuunnnn duun! Duuunnnnnnnn dun dun dun dun dun dun dun dun dun dun dunnnnnnnnnnn dunnnn …

The shark was known as a man-eating monster before *Jaws*, but the film amplified its infamy. Oscar-winning composer John Williams's dark and threatening overture is recognised the world over for its two-note bass line building to a crescendo, while Spielberg's opening sequence takes us underwater into the menacing otherworld of the shark, which looms as a shadowy presence, seen only in glimpses. We fill in the blanks. We are good at it.

From the shark gods of the Solomon Islands to the ancient mariners who believed sharks could smell impending death, we create our own logic for what we don't understand. The British Museum's 1949 *Field Book of Giant Fishes* includes a story of a shark that had been caught, gutted and thrown overboard only to be caught again on a hook baited with its own intestines. Jerome Van Croninsfield Smith's 1833 *Natural History of the Fishes of Massachusetts* reports that 'among other undigested remains' found in the stomach of a 22-foot shark 'was the headless body of a man, encased in complete armour'.

'We are not just afraid of predators,' legendary American biologist E. O. Wilson explained. 'We're transfixed by them, prone to weave stories and fables and chatter endlessly about them, because fascination creates preparedness, and preparedness, survival.'

There is a lot that we still don't understand about sharks, particularly the large, oceanic species like the great white. They may not quite be the terrifying beasts found in old library books – bloodthirsty and indestructible, prowling the deep with half-eaten, headless knights and Hebrew prophets inside – but they are wild and powerful predators that kill people. Professor Jessica Meeuwig, a conservation fellow of the Zoological Society of London and inaugural director of the Centre for Marine Futures at the University of Western Australia, pointed to Wilson's observations to explain why humans are so captivated by sharks and shark attacks.

'We do have this fascination with these big predators, whether they are bears or lions or sharks, because we don't want to be prey,' she said. 'It's fantastic that we're transforming that fascination out of fear into investment in research, so that we can better understand these animals.'

Scientists have learnt an extraordinary amount about great white sharks in the past two decades but, as Albert Einstein suggested, the more we learn, the more we realise we don't know.

'To some degree the ocean is still that big unknown and sharks are the megafauna of that world,' Southern Cross University marine ecologist Dr Daniel Bucher explained. 'Reef sharks are actually quite well known because they are more accessible, but the big oceanic species like the great white are widely spaced across a huge area of ocean, they move around in a very unpredictable manner, they're large and they're dangerous. It takes a lot of money, big boats, and a lot of luck to research great whites.'

Yet research is happening at an unprecedented rate, with Australian, American and South African institutions among those developing or supporting new techniques to better understand large, oceanic sharks, with a particular focus on satellite tagging.

Described as a 'brute' with unpredictable behaviour by Jacques Cousteau in 1956, the great white shark has been almost impossible for scientists to study in its natural environment. The first underwater footage of a great white wasn't captured until 1965, and *Jaws* was mostly filmed with mechanical sharks. The film was supplemented by footage of real sharks shot off Dangerous Reef in South Australia's Spencer Gulf by Ron and Valerie Taylor, who used pint-sized props to ensure the shark looked enormous. Tagging of great whites began in 1974, around the same time that *Jaws* was being filmed. But it was a difficult, dangerous and somewhat unreliable way to collate data, relying on tagged sharks being re-captured.

Satellite tagging began in March 2000, with the first satellite tag attached by Australia's Commonwealth Scientific and Industrial Research Organisation (CSIRO) to a juvenile female named Heather that had been captured near Wilsons Promontory in Victoria. Heather promptly disappeared. However, the tagging of another shark, named Neale, that was tagged just after Heather, was much more successful and quickly gained a cult following in Australia, with people logging on to the CSIRO website to monitor a dotted red line that plotted his movement (the dots representing each satellite transmission).

'We've even had reports of people having sweepstakes, where they're betting to see where Neale might turn up the next time we update the website,' CSIRO shark scientist Dr Barry Bruce told the ABC's *7.30 Report*.

Neale wandered far and wide. Initially he swam back and forth through the snapper fishing grounds of Victoria's east coast before heading south, across Bass Strait, around the north-eastern tip of Tasmania and as far south as Bicheno on Tasmania's east coast. Then Neale turned around and swam back, beyond the Victorian border and along the New South Wales coast to the Solitary Islands at Coffs Harbour, covering a distance of 2946 kilometres in 129 days, before the CSIRO lost transmission.

Neale and the satellite tagging that followed rapidly expanded knowledge of great whites' movement patterns. They have since been tracked crossing the Indian Ocean from South Africa to Western Australia, covering a distance of 11,000 kilometres in 99 days, diving almost 1000 metres below the surface to waters as cold as 3 °C, and registering bursts of speed of up to 50 kilometres per hour. On average, they travel 70 to 125 kilometres per day and around 3000 kilometres per month.

Satellite and sonar/acoustic tagging has generated incredible interest in great white shark research. While much remains unknown, the growing scientific knowledge is pretty impressive nonetheless. As a species, the great white shark boasts some extraordinary attributes that would not be out of place in a Stan Lee comic book.

These traits have been refined over millions of years – the earliest known great white fossils are about 16 million years old.

For starters, its two-toned body provides highly effective camouflage, appearing dark from above and white from below. Its body is built for speed and endurance. Bands of muscle run from head to tail, driving its tail fin, which powers the shark through the water, moving like a windscreen wiper. Its skeleton is made of cartilage, which is light and highly flexible, giving it extraordinary mobility. Its liver contains a special oil called squalene that is six times lighter than sea water, enabling the shark to adjust its buoyancy (a great white's enormous liver can account for as much as a quarter of its weight).

A great white shark never sleeps. It is in a perpetual state of motion, as it has to keep water moving over its gills to breathe. It does not have to 'think' about swimming in order to do it; the part of the shark's nervous system that coordinates swimming movements is located in its spinal cord, not its brain.

The great white also has sophisticated sensory organs. It can detect sound vibrations from a distance of 2 kilometres and can detect scent up to 5 kilometres away. A great white shark can detect a single drop of blood in the equivalent of an Olympic swimming pool. Its sense of smell is so advanced it can recognise different chemical compounds as well as the salinity of water. Its skin is covered in sensory pores, which is why it will sometimes bump into potential prey to get a 'taste' of it (i.e. determine its fat content). Its mouth and pharynx are lined with papillae and tastebuds, which may explain why surfers (and surfboards) are generally released after an exploratory bite.

The great white also has a kind of 'sixth sense': receptors sensitive to magnetic fields. Some scientists believe that sharks use these receptors to orient themselves with the earth's magnetic field. A great white tagged on South Africa's Western Cape in 2003 made occasional dives towards the ocean floor during a transoceanic crossing to Exmouth in Western Australia – seemingly to adjust her direction, like a hiker consulting a compass.

The great white is a fearsome predator befitting its reputation as the ultimate killing machine. It has night vision like a cat, can see above and below the water, and can completely withdraw its eye into the socket for protection when attacking. Its jaws open to 150 degrees (compared to a human's 45 degrees) and are lined with as many as 300 serrated, razor-sharp teeth that are up to 7.5 centimetres long. In *Jaws*, shark expert Matt Hooper described it as 'like a locomotive with a mouth full of butcher knives'. The great white's genus name, *Carcharodon*, comes from the Greek words 'karcharos', meaning sharp or jagged, and 'odous', meaning tooth. Its teeth are pointy, to facilitate the puncturing of flesh and grasping of prey, with fine, regularly spaced serrations to aid in cutting and ripping it into pieces. A great white's teeth aren't anchored to the jaw like human teeth are, but are linked via a series of stretchy ligaments, enabling increased flexibility. And while its teeth can break off relatively easily (it loses about one a week), it constantly regrows them.

The great white's jaws are reinforced by layers of mineralised cartilage that take years to develop (juvenile great whites like Neale feed mainly on fish, which don't require much jaw strength to eat), but its instinct to kill comes before it is even born.

Very little is known about the great white's mating habits and birth has never been observed, but at least 10 pregnant females have been examined or dissected. The great white shark is ovoviviparous, which means that the shark grows in an egg, which is then hatched inside the female's uterus. The shark embryos continue to develop inside the uterus until they are born. However, at an early stage of the estimated 12 to 18 month gestation period, the stronger embryos cannibalise their siblings. They eat the unfertilised eggs, which is called 'oophagy' or 'egg eating', and some researchers think they also eat the weaker embryos, which is called 'adelphophagy' and literally means 'eating one's brother'. This practice was discovered accidentally in 1948, when a researcher probing the uterus of a pregnant grey nurse shark (from the same family of sharks as the great white) was bitten on the hand by an in-utero shark pup.

3

THE DEEP, DARK DOWN BELOW

DARREN ROGERS DOES not frighten easily. He spent years as a martial arts instructor in Byron Bay and looks like the sort of guy you wouldn't want to meet in a dark alley.

'I am not a weak person,' he said. 'I don't think I'm anything special but I've had a tough life. A tough life makes you tough.'

But in the months following Tadashi's attack, Darren struggled with depression and post-traumatic stress that pushed him to the very brink.

'I didn't realise it was going to impact me so severely,' he said. 'It was such a black time. I was so lost. It pushed me right into a corner.'

It also threatened to take away the most important thing in his life.

'That doubt of if I would ever surf again was very strong. Surfing has saved my life numerous times, when I didn't have anything else. So to lose something so central to my existence, which my life completely revolved around, that pushed me to the limit.'

Darren grew up on Queensland's Gold Coast, where surfing was his escape from a troubled home life. 'When I was very young I got sent to Victoria. There were family problems and I got shipped out. Because I was from Queensland everyone asked: "Do you surf? Are you a surfer?" I was only about thirteen, had a single mum, but when I came back I was determined to start surfing. From the second I got involved it was a hundred per cent. That was my life.'

A few years later, before his fifteenth birthday, Darren ran away from home. 'I went and slept on the beach. My first jaunt out into the real world was sleeping in a surfboard cover in the bushes at Main Beach on the Gold Coast. Because my mum didn't like me doing a lot of things, as soon as I got away from that situation all I did was surf. It was my escape. That's all I wanted to do, that's all I thought about doing, and that's all I did, day in, day out.'

Darren worked night shifts in casual, dead-end jobs and spent his days chasing waves, from Burleigh Heads to Duranbah. 'It was the beginning of the eighties and the Gold Coast was a different place back then. Surfing really dominated my life. I look back and wonder what would have happened if I didn't surf. I had a rough upbringing and it's just the path life takes you on. For me, surfing was everything and the ocean was a place where I became really comfortable.'

Darren drifted south to Byron Bay and spent years shaping surfboards under the tutelage of pioneering surfboard maker Geoff McCoy, surfing alongside McCoy's creative muse, Cheyne Horan, a four-time runner-up in the surfing world championship. 'It wasn't the greatest career financially but I was surfing one to three times a day, shaping board after board after board for myself, learning, discovering, getting really deeply involved in surfboard design and trying out new things.'

He left McCoy and moved further south to Ballina, where he continues to make his own surfboards.

'I have never turned away from surfing, ever. It's been a constant thing.'

That was before Tadashi Nakahara died in his arms after being bitten in half by a great white shark at Darren's favourite surf spot. Darren remembers the day grimly.

'When I got home that day I was a mess. I couldn't sleep that night. I was lying there staring into the dark, looking into [Tadashi's] eyes. Because I was so close to his face and was staring into his eyes the whole time, that is the image that has stayed with me, burnt into my mind.

'I got up at midnight, sick of staring into the pitch black, hadn't slept a millisecond. I live by myself, so I got in the car and drove down and parked in the [Shelly Beach] car park in the dark. The tide was low and I went out and stood on the edge of the rocks. I stood there for hours in the dark just freaking out – not running around screaming, just standing there, unable to comprehend what had gone down.

'Then the water touched my toes and it felt like it was all the same water still, like a swimming pool, and that event was still contained right there in that body of water, even though the currents and whatever had washed on. The first bit of water that touched my toes felt tainted. I'd never felt that before when I touched water. Ever. Ever. I've felt freezing cold, heavy, windy, whatever, but not tainted.'

A pattern emerged – sleepless nights and regular visits to Shelly Beach. Darren began night-walking, from his home in

West Ballina to Shelly Beach then further along the coast to Skennars Head and back again – a return trip of 17 kilometres.

'I was just completely unable to sleep, unable to stay in the house, unable to get away from it, unable to stay away from it. It was a life-changing event. I would come to the beach every day and every night and just sit there and stare at the ocean for hours. I was driving back one day and stopped at Shaws Bay, which is an enclosed bay inside the [Richmond River] rock wall. It's tidal. The water seeps through the rock wall but there's no way a shark can get into the bay. I thought: "I've got to get in the water." I knew it was starting to bend my head.'

The shoreline at Shaws Bay is steep, dropping off quickly into deep water. Darren walked out through the shallows and nervously pushed out into the open water. As soon as his feet left the sand, he looked down.

'I couldn't see my legs. The water was clear but what I saw was Tadashi's injuries. My brain was playing some sort of trick on me. I looked down and what I saw was if my legs had been torn off. That was when I knew the effects were serious.'

Meanwhile, Brooke Mason's parents insisted she immediately fly home to Hobart in the aftermath of the attack.

'My parents got so freaked out they made me come home and wanted to see me alive and well,' she said. 'I was still in shock. [When] I saw Mum at the airport she just hugged me and held me. I was the next in line. They couldn't believe that I hadn't been attacked and how close a call it had been.'

But within days, Brooke flew back to Byron Bay determined to get back in the water.

'You just get so high on life with the miracle of surviving. I guess surfing is kind of a risk-taking [activity] that gives you that thrill and that adrenaline. But my head was still in such a spin. I'd lost my car keys and I didn't have a leg rope because it was around his body. I was trying to tell myself that I was all right but I wasn't sure. I got a blood nose in the shower and I got super freaked out. It was definitely hard not to think about it.'

With the help of her best friend, Leo Plaza, Brooke paddled out at Byron Bay's most popular surf break, The Pass, just three days after the attack.'

When it's super crowded you feel pretty safe. I was a bit freaked out at the start. When people were falling off I kept thinking that they'd been taken by a shark. I had to remind myself to calm down. But it was actually a really good surf. A few nice waves came right to me and it felt kind of like Tadashi had sent them. [It felt like] a bit of a memorial to celebrate his life. He would want us to keep surfing.'

Unfortunately, it wasn't that simple.

'I think I was in denial for that first month afterwards,' Brooke admitted later. 'I had terrible thoughts. I wished I had been eaten because that would've been better than seeing it and having to survive in your own head afterwards. Night after night I had dreams of different family and friends of mine, seeing them being attacked. It was the whole situation replaying itself with differ-ent people. It's crazy how your brain tries to process that trauma. There were so many conflicting emotions. There was the guilt – survivor guilt – because it was just luck that it wasn't me. There was anger, because the thing that I loved most in the world, surf-ing, had been taken from me. For months afterwards, when I was sitting out in the water I felt like a piece of bait, just waiting to get eaten; just sitting there, bobbing around. It didn't feel worth the risk. You are so vulnerable. You are nothing compared to a great white shark.'

Brooke gave up her dream of becoming a professional surfer and returned to university in Hobart.

'It made me think differently about surfing. It made me think that I don't want surfing to be my whole life. It made me realise that if I was a doctor maybe I could have saved him. It made me want to be more useful in that sort of situation. And studying medicine fills up my brain so much that it is a good coping mechanism. The scariest thing is having time to think. It is so dangerous when you've got all these terrible thoughts and images in your head. In a way I was really lucky that I could come back to Tasmania and act like it didn't happen and get on with my life. The whole experience definitely helped me wise up. I think I was a bit of a naïve kid before that. I definitely learnt a lot.'

Back in Ballina, Darren was getting some professional help. 'I hadn't really talked about it to anyone. I was living in the big house by myself. I was living in the world inside my head. So I ended up going to see someone about it and I was diagnosed with severe post-traumatic stress, like what happens to soldiers. And it was as brutal as seeing someone with their legs blown off. That's what it was like, a war zone, but at my favourite beach on a beautiful day.'

Talking about it helped.

'As hard as it was to relive the trauma, it was a turning point. I started to think about Tadashi and what he would want. Would he want me to give up surfing? Definitely not. He would want me to surf. I didn't know him but we are permanently bonded now. I breathed his last breaths.'

4

A KINGDOM
OF FEAR

AS DARREN ROGERS began his journey back into the ocean, surfing in Ballina had become a high-risk activity reserved for the brave and the crazy. Tadashi's death had been the fourth attack in five months on the northern New South Wales coast.

On 9 September 2014, British expat Paul Wilcox was killed by a great white shark while swimming at Byron Bay's Clarkes Beach, a stone's throw from one of Australia's most popular stretches of sand and only 30 kilometres north of Ballina. On 24 January 2015, a shark knocked Hamish Murray from his surfboard at Flat Rock, a well-known local surf break just a few kilometres outside Ballina. The shark dented Murray's surfboard and launched him a metre into the air, but the veteran surfer was back in the water the very next day, saying that 'Sharks are just part of [surfing].' On 8 February 2015, Byron Bay chef Jabez Reitman was bitten on the back by a 3-metre bull shark at Seven Mile Beach, midway between Byron and Ballina. The 35-year-old surfer drove himself to Byron Bay Hospital and told Sydney's *Daily Telegraph* that it was 'the price we pay for doing what we love'. The very next day, 9 February 2015, Tadashi Nakahara was attacked and killed at Shelly Beach, paying the ultimate price for his obsession.

'Surfers are fanatical; they love the water and the sensation of riding waves,' president of the Lennox-Ballina (Le-Ba) Board-riders Club, Don Munro, explained.

'But Tadashi's attack spooked everybody. Lennox and Ballina are very much a surfing community and surfing is a major part of our economy, so the ramifications were felt right through the community, by people who don't surf or even go to the beach. It spun everybody out but it was particularly close to home for everyone who surfed because a lot of surfers knew Tadashi. People stopped going in the water. Others became very, very cautious. People were definitely thinking: 'Am I going to be the next one who is going to be attacked?' Guys with families, with young kids, were driving an hour to the Gold Coast because of the shark nets up there. Sometimes there was surf and there would be no-one in the water. Surfers are pretty resilient but it got everybody scared.'

Something strange and scary was happening in Ballina. Sea surface temperatures were unusually warm throughout 2015 – several degrees above average – and consistently among the hottest in Australia, defying El Niño weather patterns. There were widespread reports of increased marine activity closer to shore, with bait balls (swarms of small fish like Australian sardines, which had rebounded after almost being wiped out by a herpes virus from 1995 to 1998) attracting larger predators, like dolphins, whales and sharks. And although there was a 'noticeable difference' in the number of people entering the water after Tadashi's attack, the number of shark sightings and shark encounters only escalated.

'If you look at the nature of shark attacks, they are rare events that do tend to occur in clusters,' marine ecologist at Southern Cross University Dr Daniel Bucher explained. 'That is usually because environmental conditions that bring sharks and humans into contact are seasonal events. If you look at the Western Australia clusters, when there were seven fatalities in three years [from 2010 to 2013], then there wasn't a fatality in Western Australia in the next two years [before a pair of fatal attacks in the space of five days in 2016]. Although they introduced some shark prevention and mitigation, like sonar buoys, those things did not lower the risk that much – environmental conditions changed and there just wasn't the sharks there.'

From the southern slopes of the McPherson Range near the Queensland border, the Richmond River cuts through an undulating patchwork of cow paddocks, cane fields and overgrown bush. Ballina crouches on the northern bank of the river as it curves like a serpent into the sea. The name of the town comes from the indigenous Bundjalung word 'bullinah', which means 'place of many oysters'. Today, Ballina is better known as the home of the Big Prawn – a giant orange crustacean with beady eyes, built to celebrate the local seafood industry and attract visitors to a Pacific Highway petrol station – and the shark attack capital of Australia's eastern seaboard.

Somewhat ironically, the Big Prawn's construction in 1989 was like a kiss of death for the local fishing fleet, which has drifted into decline ever since, hit by increased regulation and diminishing returns. Today, there are only four commercial fishing trawlers left operating out of Ballina, down from as many as 37 in the late 1980s, and the Big Prawn has been relocated to the car park of a national hardware chain. Now, the biggest growth industry in Ballina is retirement, with the number of residents over the age of 60 creeping up towards 30 per cent, earning the town a reputation as 'God's waiting room', in contrast with nearby Byron Bay's bare-foot, New Age, whale-hugging, organic yoga nirvana, where the streets are named after famous poets, writers and philosophers.

Ballina spanner-crab fisherman Cliff Corbett is not a poet. In fact, it is virtually impossible to quote Cliff due to his incredibly frequent use of profanities (think of words that rhyme with 'truck'). But the wizened fisherman's rough exterior doesn't hide his intimate knowledge of the ocean. Cliff has spent five decades on boats, fishing the length and breadth of the continent, includ-ing more than 30 years navigating the shifting sandbar at the Richmond River mouth in his crab boat.

'We've got the smallest fishing ground in Australia,' Cliff explained. 'We're closer to the continental shelf than anywhere else in Australia. We're on the edge of a wilderness, where there are monsters and critters – we don't even know what's out there – all the fish and everything else that is migrating up and down the coast, it comes up here.'

Cliff isn't crazy. The coastline between Byron Bay and Ballina bulges out into the Pacific, chewing into the continental shelf and creating a bottleneck for marine life migrating north to warmer waters or riding the Eastern Australian Current south, before it splits from the coast near Port Macquarie. A geological survey carried out by the Bureau of Mineral Resources, Geology and Geophysics in 1972 found that the shelf was unusually narrow at Ballina (around 25 kilometres in width), with a large submarine canyon 13 kilometres wide extending beyond the Richmond River mouth.

Cliff doesn't agree with the politicians ('bunch of wankers'), the NSW Department of Primary Industries ('bunch of dickheads') or the scientists ('they have no fucking idea'). Cliff agrees with Cliff, who blames the dramatic spike in shark attacks on the move to make the great white shark a protected species – which began in Tasmania in 1996 and led to full protection in Australian waters under the *Environment Protection and Biodiversity Conservation Act 1999*, which listed the great white as a vulnerable species because of evidence of a declining population, low levels of reproduction, limited local distribution and rapid decline in bycatch (the incidental capture of non-targeted marine species by commercial fisheries). Bycatch of great white sharks averaged around eight per year from 1961 to 1980, then dropped significantly to four per year between 1981 and 1990 and less than two between 1991 and 1999, when the act came into effect. However, some anecdotal evidence suggested that the number of juvenile sharks was increasing.

'It's simple,' Cliff explained. 'There are more great white sharks here because they have been protected. And I don't think people realise what they're looking after – they are prehistoric monsters. They were here before man and they'll probably be here after man. They are just like a blowfly. The buggers are everywhere. I see them all the time. They are just a big maggot with teeth. They don't have any brains – they don't know what they're doing or why they're doing it.'

A 2008 review of the Australian government's White Shark Recovery Plan concluded that it was 'not possible' to determine if the great white shark population had shown any sign of recovery since its protection in 1999. The review supported the great white's status as vulnerable, but actual population numbers are rubbery – recent CSIRO research suggested there were between 750 and 1200 adult great white sharks on Australia's eastern seaboard but there are no reliable metrics with which to compare changes in population. Scientists from the CSIRO, WA Fisheries, the NSW Department of Primary Industries and the University of Technology Sydney are currently working on the first robust population study of great white sharks in Australian waters, using genetic and statistical analysis, satellite tagging and aerial surveys. Previous research that analysed genetic material dating back to 1989 found that there were two distinct great white shark populations – an eastern population (from the east coast of Tasmania to central Queensland) and a western population (from the west coast of Victoria to north-west Western Australia) that did not interact, with Bass Strait acting as a barrier for both.

'Our tagging and tracking showed that white sharks travel thousands of kilometres,' CSIRO's Dr Barry Bruce said in a statement. 'But sharks tagged and tracked off eastern Australia did not go west of Bass Strait, and sharks tagged off Western and South Australia rarely went east.'

In 2004, the Convention on International Trade in Endangered Species of Wild Fauna and Flora (CITES) suggested that the global population of great white sharks had declined by at least 20 per cent over the last three generations. However, Lennox Head fisherman Paul Morrissey has witnessed a dramatic increase in the number of great whites on the northern New South Wales coast in the past decade.

'It's multiplying all the time,' Paul said. 'Previously, you might see an odd one but now they are around all the time.'

Paul, who retired in 2015 after 33 years as a commercial fisherman, believes the increased number of great white sharks is linked to the creation of the Australian Whale Sanctuary in 1999. (Whaling has been banned in Australia since the introduction of the *Whale Protection Act 1980*, and numbers have rebounded to near pre-whaling levels.) Large sharks follow the humpback whales migrating north. Paul thinks that the establishment of the Cape Byron Marine Park in 2002, which extends from the Brunswick River to Lennox Head and covers an area of around 22,000 hectares, provides these sharks with a local food source.

'I believe the decline of commercial fishing and the restrictions and the protections have got a lot to do with the increase in attacks,' he said. 'The longer it goes on, the more dangerous it's going to become. The number of sharks is just increasing, increasing all of the time, while the commercial fishing is only decreasing. I'm not a conservationist. I've spent the biggest percentage of my life on the water, so in my books I've got just as much right to be there as they have. But you would not get me swimming [in the ocean] now after what I've seen. I've seen too many sharks. I'd be scared of a shadow.'

'There is a shark expert on every street corner in Ballina,' Don Munro said.

The midweek shoppers at Ballina Central are bursting with theories, extending beyond the usual 'warm water, more baitfish, more sharks' hypotheses, with many acutely aware of the decline of the local fishing industry and the impact of the Cape Byron Marine Park (which one local described as 'a McDonald's drive-through for sharks'). Climate change is discussed in earnest, as is the influence of an unusually strong El Niño season, a later-than-usual migration of humpback whales, tidal patterns linked to lunar cycles and increasing coastal populations ('there's that many surfers up here now, it's crazy'). Conspiracy theories are aired by hi-vis-clad tradies queuing outside Zaza Kebabs, about whale carcasses buried in sand dunes and a shiver of half a dozen 'problem' sub-adult sharks loitering at the Richmond River mouth like a gang of teenage thugs.

'I think it is an accumulation of a series of different things but I don't think anyone really knows,' said Don, a wiry veteran of 30 summers surfing this stretch of coast. 'You're talking about a highly evolved animal and to know the reasons why they do what they do is impossible.'

Generally speaking, there is a scientific answer to everything. The exceptions, it would seem, include ghosts, zombies and killer sharks.

'You can look at things that correlate,' Dr Daniel Bucher explained. 'We've looked at the Surf Life Saving Australia records and the number of times they spotted a shark or closed the beach because of a shark presence, and it did show that there was some correlation with things like rainfall, water temperature and the Southern Oscillation Index [El Niño]. In the summer of 2014/2015, the spike [of shark attacks] had really started to happen, so something in that year made it an outlier.

'I think we had a strong El Niño year, so the south-east trade winds weren't blowing as strongly, but the usual pattern is that the water should be cooler. There weren't any big storm events. That meant that the sand that was usually washed away from the beaches by storms built up and we ended up with big sandbars close to shore with a deep channel in front of it. That meant that the sharks could actually come in closer to the beach than they normally would.

'The schools of baitfish that would normally get broken up by those storms accumulated into these huge rafts, which attracted not only sharks, but there was a lot of dolphin activity and there was a lot of whale activity. So we think it was a combination of calm conditions and warm water, but I don't think there [were] necessarily more sharks than normal – they were closer to shore than normal, so we saw them and interacted with them more.'

As people argued over competing theories, the shark attacks continued. On 11 March 2015, Byron Bay fisherman Robbie Graham was knocked backwards into the water when a 'huge' great white shark charged his tinny while he was fishing for tuna near Julian Rocks, less than 3 kilometres offshore from Byron Bay. The dramatic incident resulted in the closure of Byron's main beach and forced tourist operators to cancel water-based activities.

On 2 July 2015, Ballina bodyboarder Matt Lee was attacked by a great white shark at the southern end of Lighthouse Beach, at a popular surf break known as North Wall due to its proximity to the Richmond River rock wall, and just a few hundred metres south of where Tadashi was taken. In an eerie echo of Tadashi's attack, the 32-year-old had his legs savagely mauled and was incredibly lucky to survive, thanks largely to the quick thinking of fellow surfers who pulled him from the water and applied a tourniquet to his legs, a retiree walking on the beach who called triple-0, and the rapid arrival of a rescue helicopter from the Gold Coast.

The timing of the attack could not have been worse. The world's largest junior surfing competition was scheduled to start at nearby Lennox Head the very next day.

'Surfing has an enormous input into the local economy and that event is the biggest money spinner, tourist-wise,' Don Munro explained.

Things quickly went from bad to worse. On the morning of the event, a shark knocked Surfers Paradise teacher Mike Hoile off his surfboard at Lennox Point, leaving a trail of teeth marks along the bottom of his board.

'We closed everything down for twenty-four hours,' Ballina mayor David Wright said.

'We had a thousand people in town so we couldn't afford for [the junior surfing competition] not to go ahead. We got extra rubber duckies [inflatable rubber boats] and we employed Australian Aerial Patrol and Air T&G to fly their helicopter. It ended up costing sixteen thousand dollars for the five days, but we didn't see a shark.'

Over the next few months, the Ballina mayor acted as a lightning rod for a frightened, angry and confused community unsure of what to do about the intensifying 'shark problem'.

'It's not really the council's jurisdiction but everyone that saw me wanted to talk about sharks,' he said.

'It was definitely affecting the economy and the mood of the community. People were afraid to go in the water, unable to do what they loved doing, and I certainly felt a sense of responsibility. After Matt [Lee], I lived in fear of another attack. I do a lot of walking. I was going walking earlier and earlier because I kept thinking: "There's going to be another attack."

'We had whales very close to the beach, dolphins and huge bait balls – it was like someone had spilled a great big bottle of Indian ink in the water. It could be two hundred to three hundred metres long and a hundred metres wide, with dolphins and sharks going through it feeding, but the actual shape of the thing didn't change. When the DPI [Department of Primary Industries] flew over in the helicopter the first time, they saw seven sharks and more than fifty dolphins in the mouth of the river. The amount of baitfish was unbelievable. They said it was the greatest aggregation of sea life they'd ever seen in one place at one time.'

It was a near-fatal combination. On 31 July 2015, a 4-metre great white shark attacked Craig Ison while he was surfing at Evans Head, 40 kilometres south of Ballina. The shark took a huge chunk out of Craig's left thigh, severing his leg just millimetres from his femoral artery, and it was only the former boxer's fighting instincts that saved his life.

'It was personal,' Craig told *The Daily Telegraph*.

> [The shark] was saying to me: 'Don't even bother thinking you're going to get out of this one mate, you're fucked.' But I said to the shark: 'Fuck you, I'll fight dirty too.' His jaws were just ripping and tearing and I'm there just looking at it. I thought: 'I better do something.' So I went 'bang, bang, bang, bang' and punched him four times and he let go. He would have just kept going, fucking at my leg until my leg dropped off, if I didn't punch him.

After waking from an induced coma, the 52-year-old, who fought world featherweight champion Jeff Fenech in the early 1980s, declared that his surfing days were done.

> There are that many sharks, it's ridiculous. It's all about numbers, and when you have protected a species like [the] killer white shark for fifteen years, what do you think is going to happen? The numbers are going to grow and they're going to attack. There's no way I'm getting back in the water. No way in the world. I managed to beat a white pointer. That'll do me.

Ballina felt like a community under siege, like a modern-day Amity Island, with mayor David Wright brushing off media comparisons to both police chief Martin Brody and venal Amity Island mayor Larry Vaughn. Unlike Brody's brooding tough guy, David is a small, nervy man with a shock of pure white hair who teaches the talented and gifted class at Alstonville Public School, 14 kilometres inland from Ballina. On 10 August, more than 200 people crammed into a tiny hall in Lennox Head, angry and frustrated by the lack of action by local and state governments.

'The mood was very, very agitated,' Don Munro said. 'The mayor was invited to speak and he was heckled.'

In a show of hands, about 95 per cent of attendees voted for a shark cull and threatened to take matters into their own hands if something wasn't done.

'We'd had enough,' Don said. 'The situation was diabolical. We're talking about people's lives and livelihoods. It was an unprecedented crisis. Surfers are more environmentally aware than most. We live in the water, we have an appreciation that we're in [the sharks'] domain, but it had just gone crazy.'

Only six months earlier, in the wake of Tadashi's attack, Don had cautioned against a shark cull.

'None of us were into culling, myself in particular, but we'd got to a desperate situation,' he explained. 'There were enough incidents for the government to get off its arse and do something, but it hadn't and it wasn't. So we indicated to them: "This [culling sharks] is what we think you should do." If they weren't prepared to do the job, we knew guys that were.'

PART TWO

5

THE GREAT WHITE SHARK HUNTER

THE OLD MAN was thin and gaunt with deep wrinkles on the back of his neck. He sat at the stern of a small red-and-white fishing boat moored on a block of blue concrete, with a fibreglass shark floating overhead, its jaws agape. Behind him was the infamous Shark Show bearing his name – a lurid tourist attraction on Hervey Bay's esplanade, where entry was through a set of gigantic toothy jaws.

Beside the entrance was a wall emblazoned with a faded image from long ago, of a younger man with a moustache and wide smile crouched beside a very large shark, hooked through the nose like an ancient Assyrian, blood streaking its lower jaw. It was a memorial of sorts, immortalising the moment almost 30 years before, when the old man was a hero. Vic Hislop, the great white shark hunter, had been celebrated around the globe for wrestling a fishing rod for three hours in stormy seas and gale force winds to drag a 'world record' killer from the depths of the Southern Ocean: a 6.2-metre monster weighing almost two-and-a-half tonnes. Inside, the star attraction was another giant, only slightly smaller, caught just off the Queensland coastline, before the great white became a protected species. It was frozen, with jaws pried wide open, fated to elicit gasps of wonder from Japanese tourists rather than roam the ocean deep.

'There are a lot of animals and other things that need our protection in this world but the great white shark has never been one of them,' the old man said, gazing wistfully towards the flat horizon, where ferries and whale watching tours floated out across the sandy estuary towards Fraser Island. 'They're not teddy bears. They're man-eaters.'

Vic Hislop belongs to that great Australian pantheon of self-made adventure heroes alongside Alby Mangels and Troy Dann – their swashbuckling, alpha-male achievements tainted somewhat by the unmistakable whiff of self-promotion. Yet at the height of Hislop's fame, in the late 1980s, few captured the country's imagination quite like the straight-talking Queensland shark hunter. He would drag *Jaws*, his aptly named aluminium shark boat, to all corners of the continent, arriving at the scene of an attack armed with his homemade fishing gear and a wild-eyed, steely resolve to catch the killer responsible. Crowds of people would flock to coastal jetties and piers to watch Vic return triumphant and unload another monster catch, like the afore-mentioned 6.2-metre 'world record' shark caught near Phillip Island in Victoria in November 1987.

'I feel no guilt when I catch a fish like this,' he said in his 1993 book, *Vic Hislop Shark Man*.

They are just killing machines, the great white and the tiger shark. They maim and kill twenty-four hours a day.

They are just tonnes of muscle with a big mouth and razor sharp teeth.

Vic Hislop was born in 1947 in the small country town of Stanthorpe in the granite belt of southern Queensland, north of Tenterfield and about 220 kilometres inland from Ballina. When he was seven years old his family moved to the waterside Brisbane suburb of Redcliffe, in the middle of the peninsula of the same name, which juts out into the shallow waters of Moreton Bay. Young Vic was drawn to the shimmering bay, an oversized, 150,000-hectare lagoon that lies inside a collection of sand islands – Bribie, Moreton and North and South Stradbroke. The curious youngster soon developed a love of fishing and a deep interest in sharks.

'Sharks have been my life since I was twelve,' he said. 'That's when I spotted one gliding through the water for the first time. Thankfully, I was on the shore – and I was transfixed.'

At the age of 13, Vic's father built him a canoe. He painted a shark's mouth on the bow – blood red with jagged, pointy teeth. That same year, in July 1960, the trawler *Halkin* sank in Pearl Channel, the northern passage of Moreton Bay. Wreckage was strewn along the Queensland coast, from Noosa to Bribie Island, but the seven men aboard were never seen again.

'All they found were a few body parts washed up on the island,' Vic recalled.

'Our school looked out across Moreton Bay and I'd sit there thinking: "What could do this to those big, strong men?" The water always looked so calm and peaceful. That was bad enough, but when a doctor friend of my father lost both his legs in shallow water, I decided to learn more about killer sharks. That was the start of it for me. It was a mystery and I had to find out as much as I could.'

Hislop caught his first shark when he was 14 years old – a bronze whaler that towed his canoe around Moreton Bay until it eventually tired and Vic hauled it out of the water, draping it across the bow of his canoe.

'It was a scary experience, but when I finally got him it was a big moment.'

Like the shark, Vic was hooked. He began hiring bigger boats to catch bigger fish.

'As the years went by the sharks I caught got larger and my thirst for knowledge became more intense. A lot of people thought I was a little crazy in those days, towing in such huge sharks in rough weather with small boats.'

Then, in March 1977, he embarked on his first high-profile 'shark hunt'.

Just before midnight on Friday 11 March 1977, the Brisbane-bound Japanese freighter *Shun Oh* collided with a fishing boat in Moreton Bay, slicing the smaller vessel in half and throwing all three men aboard into the water. The men (all related through marriage) clung to a splintered icebox, drifting through the night, all the next day and into the early hours of Sunday morning, when a large tiger shark appeared. The shark nudged the icebox, circling and terrorising the men, before dragging its first victim, well-known local game fisherman Victor Beaver, into the water.

'Goodbye mates, this is it,' Beaver shouted before disappearing into the depths.

Then the shark returned, biting off the arm of Beaver's son-in-law, John Hayes. Somehow Hayes scrambled back onto the icebox, where his brother-in-law, Verdon Harrison, applied a tourniquet to his bleeding limb. But the shark had smelt blood.

'It's got my foot,' Hayes screamed as he was dragged underwater.

By this stage, a charter boat had spotted the blue icebox bobbing in the ocean, but the shark wasn't finished yet.

'I tried to climb into the icebox for safety, but this big shark tried to climb in with me,' Harrison told United Press International. 'Just then my rescuers came along. How I escaped I'll never know. It was a bloody nightmare.'

Harrison was taken to Royal Brisbane Hospital suffering from exposure and bites to his lower legs.

Vic and Jim Beer from the Moreton Bay Boat Club spent the next night trawling the area where the two fishermen had been taken, using stingrays as bait. After a long, sleepless night, at around 6.30 am, Vic hooked a 5.2-metre tiger shark in the very same corner of Moreton Bay where the men had disappeared.

'I had hunted sharks in this area for years, but had never seen anything of this enormous bulk before,' he said.

'I knew that was the shark. Not just because of the size or because it was in the same spot one night later, but I had a sixth sense – as soon as I looked at it and especially when I touched it. It was the first time I felt *the feeling*. It's hard to describe being in the exact spot within hours of where humans have been torn apart by a creature that you alone know too well. You can imagine only too vividly exactly what took place.'

The catch made headlines around the globe: 'Killer shark slain', Arizona's *Tucson Daily Citizen* declared. And a star was born. Almost overnight, Vic Hislop had become a world famous shark hunter.

Two years later, in September 1979, Vic cemented his reputation by catching an enormous great white shark with the girth of a minibus. The 5.2-metre beast weighed 2.25 tonnes and took four hours to be hauled onto dry land.

'I had to get it ashore alive to embalm it and had to have everything ready when we landed,' he explained.

He quickly declared it was 'the largest shark ever landed in the world' and put the embalmed specimen on display, charging people $1.50 ($1 for children) to 'Gaze into the Maw of Eternity'. The shark show was popular, reflecting our ongoing fascination with apex predators and creatures of the deep. Vic bought a caravan and took the show on the road, driving south from Caloundra to Tweed Heads, Coffs Harbour, Sydney, Wollongong and Canberra, where he set up at the entrance to Belconnen Mall. (The mall was then the southern hemisphere's largest shopping centre, complete with travelators and multistorey car parks.) The cultured class of Australia's capital city was less than impressed with the spectacle.

'Perhaps I am mad but I think it is a shame that the showbiz slaughter of sharks should be commended,' columnist Ian Warden opined in *The Canberra Times* in February 1982.

It saddens me to see people gathered around a dead shark regarding it rather as the plain people of London used to regard a defused bomb during the Blitz, with a mixture of horror, relief and triumph. And when I see some smirking game fisherman standing beside a dead marlin dangled upside down, which he has just hounded to death and plucked from its happy home, I wish that someone would kick him off the wharf and that he would fall into the jaws of *Jaws*.

By 1982, the terror of *Jaws* had faded. The sequel had flopped and there was a growing awareness, both in Australia and worldwide, of conservation and environmental issues. Yet Vic Hislop was still acting like Quint, Amity Island's borderline-crazy harpoon-wielding, shark-hating fisherman, dragging his nails down the chalkboard to gain attention, hunting down 'bad fish' and then putting them on display: 'the head, the tail, the whole damn thing'. Hislop's actions were becoming increasingly controversial.

But it hadn't always been so. Sharks have been fished since time immemorial: called from the deep with ancient songs and chants, caught with lassos and bone hooks, their flesh eaten, their teeth used as weapons or tools, their skin used to cover the hilts of samurai swords, toiletry cases and mid-eighteenth-century French fashion accessories. Their jaws became souvenirs, their carcasses fertiliser, their fins ingredients in soup and traditional Chinese medicines, their liver oil used in cosmetics and haemorrhoid cream. Once upon a time, the Vic Hislops of the world were simply making a living, away from the limelight, dissecting the sharks they caught for cat food, rust protectant, souvenirs and jewellery.

Catching monster sharks wasn't enough. Vic may have enjoyed the fame and the fawning crowds of suburban mums and dads, but his obsession seems, more than anything, driven by deeply held beliefs about the dangers of big sharks. He explained in *Vic Hislop Shark Man*:

> I feel the need to enlighten people and make them aware that
> while we continue to deplete the oceans of the sharks' food

source, we will see large dangerous sharks coming closer to shore, resulting in the loss of more human lives.

In some small way, I am helping Mother Nature keep a balance in an area where man has thinned everything out except the end of the food chain – the large dangerous shark.

Hislop became a crusader who raged against the 'cover-up' of shark attacks and blamed a 'small-minded minority' who pushed for the protection of great white sharks without robust evidence about population numbers and often for 'their own commercial gain'.

'There's a huge cover-up surrounding the real number of people killed by sharks in Australia,' he said in a 2009 interview with UK newspaper *The Sun*.

The power of the dollar is put before human life. Officials don't want to jeopardise the tourist industry by revealing the true extent of fatal shark attacks. They don't investigate anything. Unless someone actually sees a victim being eaten, it's put down to drowning. At least a hundred swimmers disappear every year [in Australia] and their bodies are never found. Many have been eaten. I've caught sharks and removed human hands and feet from their stomachs … [In total] I've found human remains in ten sharks over the years and handed the evidence to police, but I've never heard another thing.

As the 1980s progressed, Vic Hislop's provocative rhetoric matched the upward trajectory of the Rubik's Cube. He became more and more outspoken, waging a one-man war on killer sharks and their public allies, particularly cage dive operator Rodney Fox and underwater filmmakers Ron and Valerie Taylor.

'A lot of people disagree with my ideas, but I know they're true,' he said.

If it wasn't for me, people would be ready to have white pointers as pets. The idea that sharks need protecting has just been pushed and pushed in the media for years, and now many people believe that this is the case. In truth, sharks in Australian waters were never really protected for conservation purposes. They have been protected wholly and solely for one thing – cage diving. And this cage diving is putting us all at risk. Make no mistake: these sharks are being trained every year to eat people thanks to cage diving.

'Sharks, right from when they are little, come across blood scents, whether it be from whales, packs of dolphins or turtles being killed and ripped apart by other sharks,' Vic explained in *The Sydney Morning Herald* in 2012.

They follow this scent along the current to the source. As they get closer, their senses get more and more aroused, and then they attack whatever is on the end of that line of scent. So as sharks follow the berley trail left by cage dive operators, the same thing happens – they get more and more excited. And at the end of this trail what does the shark see? Humans in cages. The shark then immediately associates humans with food and berley. What cage diving has done has put us right in that particular shark's food chain.

As attitudes to the marine environment changed, Vic became entangled in ever more complex fishing regulations. In 1985, when 33-year-old mother of four Shirley Durdin was bitten in half while snorkelling with her husband and children at Port Lincoln in South Australia, Vic arrived within days, driving fifty hours nonstop from Queensland to promise Shirley's husband that he would catch the shark that killed his wife. Instead, South Australian authorities confiscated Hislop's equipment and charged him with intent to fish in the Spencer Gulf fishing zone without a permit.

In September 1987, when professional diver Terry Gibson disappeared while diving for scallops off Marino Rocks in Adelaide's south, Vic was lobbied by a group of local businessmen to catch the 3-metre great white shark that had been spotted in the area in the weeks before Gibson vanished. (A buoyancy vest and weight belt, showing severe damage consistent with a shark attack, were recovered by water police but Gibson's body was never found.) But again Hislop fell foul of South Australian authorities, who destroyed the lines he had set (baited with eagle rays flown in from Kangaroo Island), confiscated his equipment and charged him for fishing without a permit. In a sign of the changing times, Gibson's wife, Lynette, backed the authorities, saying that she and her five children did not want the shark hunted down and killed.

'Sharks are part of nature,' Lynette Gibson told *The Canberra Times*. 'I think by going and saying to kill them, then you're giving human qualities to an animal that is only out there trying to survive.'

These public setbacks would have surely tested the resolve of a lesser (and less obsessive) man, but Vic Hislop was dogged in his pursuit of the monsters of the deep. He had recently established his 'savagely realistic' Shark Show at Hervey Bay, declaring it 'a factual show that injects some sanity and reality about the dangerous [shark] species'. He had bought and refitted a refrigerated truck from a meatworks in Townsville, having 'decided to catch the largest great white shark ever' and freeze it for posterity. Less than two months after the Marino Rocks fiasco, Vic was contacted by the management of the Phillip Island Fairy Penguin Reserve, who were concerned that sharks were responsible for a recent drop in penguin numbers.

'I was not surprised. I told them I had once caught a shark with thirteen penguins in its stomach.'

Vic had always wanted to fish for great white sharks off Phillip Island, on the edge of Bass Strait, that boisterous body of water separating Tasmania from mainland Australia. And for three days and three nights, he got his wish. Along with his 20-year-old son, Brett, and 16-year-old deckhand Dean Newell, Vic battled the spume and spray of the wind-tossed sea near Seal Rocks, a low-lying rocky outcrop about a kilometre off the western tip of Phillip Island and home to one of Australia's largest fur seal colonies.

'We were like drowned rats, with waves breaking over the top of the boat continuously,' he recalled.

At 5.30 am, in the grey light of the fourth morning, with the crew 'very discouraged' and at its lowest ebb, an enormous great white shark finally took the bait: a 300-pound greasy rock cod threaded through a 600-centimetre shark hook. For the next three hours, Vic and the monstrous shark were locked in the fight of their lives. The shark was bigger than his 6-metre boat, which in turn was being buffeted by gale-force winds and giant waves. Vic would let the line run at the crest of each swell before slowly inching the shark back towards the boat. The 2.5-tonne shark would drag the boat backwards, pulling the stern under and flooding the deck. 'It started to get quite hairy. We half filled with water. Even with two bilge pumps going and two strong young men bailing, there was still a lot of water in the boat all the time.'

It was a close-run thing, but eventually Vic had the shark up next to the boat. 'I will never forget that moment. The enormous bulk – it was longer than our boat and rounder and definitely a lot more solid. It was as if you could step out of the boat onto a small island. It gave us a hell of a hiding – it was going crazy.'

By 9 am, he had the tail roped. By 11.30 am, he was back at the sheltered boat ramp at Cowes, surrounded by hundreds of exuberant onlookers and hailed as a hero. By the next day, the famous image of Vic posing beside the dead beast in his chocolate-brown stubbies, Poona Palms Caravan Park t-shirt and wide, satisfied smile would be splashed across the front page of newspapers around the world. As he recalled in his book:

> That shark was the toughest I had ever faced. I had 30 years of experience and wouldn't have liked trying with anything less. As I was doing battle [with the shark], I couldn't help reflecting on all the people who had gone missing in this area. I had always wanted to fish there since our former prime minister Harold Holt went missing [at Cheviot Beach, near Portsea, around 20 nautical miles west of Seal Rocks]. Since then well over 100 people have vanished in this same area. Death certificates all read: 'considered drowned, no body recovered'. I wondered if this [shark] had taken any.

While Vic's moment of glory was still warm, the critics circled, questioning his 'world record' claims and decrying his killing of a 'defenceless' animal. And, despite an invitation from Australian Sporting Records, Hislop did not submit an application, statutory declaration or supporting verification about the record catch.

'He has refused in the past to give any professional ichthy-ologist [fish scientist] the opportunity to measure his world records, several of which he has claimed over the years,' Queensland Museum's curator of fishes, renowned marine biologist R.J. McKay, said dismissively in *The Sydney Morning Herald*.

The environmentalists and conservationists were equally unimpressed.

'Many people are appalled at the killing of defenceless wildlife, which he epitomises,' long-serving Queensland Conservation Council coordinator Liz Bourne told *The Sydney Morning Herald*. 'Sharks are major predators at the top of the food chain. They should be respected by humans, not subjected to savagery.'

Ultimately, the conservationists prevailed. Vic was banned from fishing in Victoria and South Australia. A decade after his monumental catch at Phillip Island, the great white shark was made a protected species in Tasmania, Victoria, Queensland, New South Wales, Western Australia and South Australia, and two years later, in 1999, federal legislation was introduced protecting the species in all Commonwealth waters. That was a 'sad day for all the gentle creatures in the ocean', Hislop said bitterly. It was certainly a sad day for Vic Hislop. However, by then the shark hunter had opened another shark show at Airlie Beach in North Queensland, in 1996. He had also accumulated countless freezers full of specimens.

'What's weird about that?' he asked journalist Annabel Crabb in *The Sunday Age* in 2006. 'You keep a spare tyre for your car? Well, I keep a spare great white.'

The spare sharks came in handy when budding young British artist Damien Hirst came knocking in 1991, hoping to procure something 'big enough to eat you'. Hirst was a virtually unknown art graduate ('a mixed-up young nobody with a tank full of formaldehyde and a dream', according to Crabb), when he contacted the legendary Queensland shark hunter. The 4.3-metre tiger shark Hislop supplied became *The Physical Impossibility of Death in the Mind of Someone Living* – one of the most iconic artworks of the 1990s and emblematic of the Young British Artists movement.

Preserved in 16,500 litres of formaldehyde in a glass tank, the shark was exhibited at the Saatchi Gallery in 1992 and earned Hirst a nomination for the prestigious Turner Prize. Like Hislop, it was endlessly controversial. Australian-born art critic Robert Hughes declared it a 'cultural obscenity'.

It was a profitable one if nothing else. The cofounder of the influential Saatchi & Saatchi advertising agency, Charles Saatchi, had commissioned the artwork for around $100,000. Hirst had reportedly bought the shark from Hislop for $10,000. In 2004, Saatchi sold it to billionaire Wall Street hedge fund manager Steven A. Cohen for a reported US$8 million. When the original shark began to deteriorate, Hislop supplied Hirst with a replacement, which was then exhibited at the Metropolitan Museum of Art in New York from 2007 to 2010. *The New York Times* art critic Roberta Smith described the shark as 'simultaneously life and death incarnate in a way you don't quite grasp until you see it, suspended and silent, in its tank'.

'It seems to surge forward, ready to pounce on some unseen prey just beyond the tank,' Smith said. 'If you bend down and peer through its sharply jagged teeth, you'll be looking past the pure white mouth at the large black hole of its gullet. It's a reasonable visual metaphor for the crossing-over that we think will never happen.'

It is what Vic Hislop had described decades earlier as gazing into 'the Maw of Eternity'. More than anyone, Hislop has long understood the grisly appeal of the killer sharks he caught. Yet even his wild imagination would never have predicted that this primal appeal would transfer from a caravan of horrors touring the landlocked country towns of Australia to the finest museums and galleries of Europe and North America.

During a collaboration spanning two decades, Hislop filled shipping containers with frozen hammerhead, bull, tiger and great white sharks, which Hirst transformed into multimillion-dollar works of art. In March 2006, the Samsung Museum in Seoul bought a pickled tiger shark entitled *The Wrath of God* for $5.7 million. In September 2008, another tiger shark, which Hirst named *The Kingdom*, sold for more than £9.6 million at a Sotheby's auction. He unveiled two more pickled sharks at a solo exhibition at the Oceanographic Museum of Monaco in 2010: a hammerhead he called *Fear of Flying* and a great white titled *The Immortal*.

'It blows my mind,' Vic confessed. 'It's out of my league. I just catch sharks. [But] I have to admit that when I see pictures of his work, I pinch myself and think: "That's one of mine." It's brilliant.'

But without the famous artist's name attached, Vic has had far less success selling his trophy catches. In December 2015, he tried to sell a frozen 5-metre great white shark for $30,000 on online classifieds website Gumtree.

'Now is your chance to own it and reap the rewards as a traveling display or use our [*sic*] imagination even pride and joy in your mancave,' the Gumtree ad read, in the typical 'tortured grammar' described by keen Hislop watcher Frank Robson.

The shark in question had been the star attraction at his Airlie Beach Shark Show, which closed its doors in 2006, condemning the behemoth to an afterlife in a refrigerated trailer in Vic's backyard.

'It is pretty hard to get rid of something like that,' Vic told *Riptide* magazine's Michael Saunders. 'It has cost me thousands of dollars in electricity to keep.'

Although Hislop maintained that he had caught the shark in 1988, before the great white became a protected species, Gumtree removed the advertisement for breaching its wildlife trade policy. Shark conservationist and underwater filmmaker Madison Stewart reported the attempted sale to the Queensland Department of Agriculture and Fisheries.

'It is crazy,' Madison said. 'I thought someone as experienced as [Vic Hislop] would know that it was illegal to sell [a great white shark].'

But Vic remained hopeful of offloading the frozen monster: 'A bloke rang me from China and wanted to know about it. But I don't think I will go through the trouble of trying to send it to China.'

In February 2016, faced with falling visitor numbers and rising maintenance costs, Vic Hislop closed his infamous shark show at Hervey Bay. After 40 years 'battling for the truth to come out' and leading the shark cull debate in Australia, Vic declared time and shut up shop.

'It's time for it to come to an end and it is sad,' he told ABC Wide Bay radio. 'I have finally made up my mind that that's it, I'll get on and do some other things now. I'm a bit upset about it. It's a lifetime of work.'

But make no mistake: Vic Hislop still holds strong views about the dangers of big sharks. 'Ending the protection of shark species would be the best thing to happen to the ecosystem. The world cannot continue to thin out the entire food chain without thinning the end-of-the-line predator, and that is exactly what is happening.'

But the small red-and-white fishing boat, stuck on a block of blue concrete on the edge of an empty car park, is going nowhere.

'It's not going to get better,' the old man warned ominously. 'It's going to get worse.'

6

THE YEAR OF THE SHARK

NUMBERS DO NOT lie. 2015 was a record year for the number of unprovoked shark attacks worldwide. The International Shark Attack File investigated 164 incidents and recorded 98 unprovoked shark attacks (aggressive interactions initiated by sharks against humans). That figure was 30 per cent above the yearly average, 26 more than in 2014 and 10 more than the previous high of 88, recorded in 2000. Six of the attacks were fatal, which was twice as many as the year before.

'Sharks plus humans equals attacks,' according to George Burgess, a bespectacled, bushy-bearded George R.R. Martin doppelgänger. Director of the University of Florida's shark research program, Burgess has also overseen the world's longest running database on shark attacks (the International Shark Attack File) at the Florida Museum of Natural History for the past 20 years.

'As our population continues to rapidly grow and shark populations slowly recover, we're going to see more interactions.

We can and should expect the number of attacks to be higher each year. When we visit the sea, we're on their turf,' he explained in a statement released by the University of Florida. 'That's the fundamental problem with shark attacks and human perception of shark attacks,' Burgess continued.

> We tend to forget that when we enter the sea, we're entering a foreign environment … We can't breathe underwater. When we enter the sea, it's a wilderness experience. In any wilderness experience, there are potential dangers to be involved in that environment. Luckily for us, the sea is a pretty benevolent place. Each year, millions of people enter the sea and come out unscratched and unscathed and oblivious to the notion that they've had a wilderness experience. But we all need to remember that, especially if we go in areas where large predators such as great white sharks live.

Somewhat surprisingly, the US experienced more than 75 per cent of all unprovoked shark attacks worldwide in 2015. There were 59 attacks in the US, with more than half of those in Florida, which accounted for more than 30 per cent of the global total. However, *fatal* shark attacks in Florida are rare. On average, one person is killed every 10 years. The last fatality was in 2010, when 38-year-old Stephen Schafer bled to death after being bitten on his right thigh while kiteboarding off Florida's Treasure Coast. While Florida has experienced an upsurge in shark attacks in the past four years, most are 'hit-and-run' attacks: cases of mistaken identity, generally perpetrated by relatively smaller blacktip and spinner sharks in shallow, murky water. Burgess described these attacks as 'the equivalent of a dog bite'.

'Those are the species involved in the occasional nips, but they are not man-eaters,' he explained.

Tiger sharks, on the other hand, *are* man-eaters. Solitary creatures with an unpredictable and often aggressive temperament, tiger sharks are second only to the great white as the species responsible for the greatest number of human fatalities. Named for the dark stripes that adorn its body when juvenile, the tiger shark (*Galeocerdo cuvier*) can grow to as long as 5.5 metres and weigh as much as 800 kilograms.

The tiger shark is the apex predator in tropical waters and is implicated in almost every serious shark attack in Hawaii, of which there were seven in 2015, including the only fatality in American waters. On 29 April 2015, a tiger shark mauled 65-year-old snorkeller Margaret Cruse near the southern tip of the island of Maui, about 200 metres offshore of local surf spot Dumps, not far from Mākena Beach. Cruse was the third person to be killed by a tiger shark in the Mākena area in the space of three years. On 14 August 2013, a tiger shark bit the right arm off 20-year-old German tourist Jana Lutteropp while she was snorkelling 100 metres off nearby Palauea Beach. Lutteropp died in hospital a week later. On 2 December 2013, a tiger shark bit the right foot off 57-year-old retired Boeing engineer Patrick Briney, whose leg was dangling in the water while he fished from a kayak about 800 metres off Mākena State Park. Briney was dead within hours.

The shark (*mano*), and the tiger shark (*niuhi*) in particular, inhabits a unique place in Hawaiian culture. Ancient Hawaiians worshipped shark gods and, traditionally, sharks have been identified as reincarnated ancestors (*aumakua*) who act as guardians to protect family members from harm (like Moana's grandmother Tala's spirit taking the shape of an illuminated manta ray in the 2016 Disney film *Moana*), often appearing in dreams as omens of both good and evil. The latter fits with the shark's other, more modern manifestation as a ferocious predator, feared by surfers and swimmers across the Hawaiian archipelago. A recent spike in shark attacks has only heightened this image. There were 53 unprovoked shark attacks in Hawaiian waters from 2012 to 2016, with the average number of attacks per year skyrocketing to more than double Hawaii's 20-year average.

University of Hawaii marine biologist Carl Meyer, who has co-authored various studies of the movement patterns, distribution and diet of tiger sharks in the Hawaiian islands, said it was virtually impossible to explain the recent increase in attacks.

'It's very, very difficult, perhaps impossible, to join the dots in a way that would be satisfactory, at least from a scientific perspective,' Meyer explained to *Outside* magazine.

What you tend to have is a typically low number of shark attacks and over time you might see some spikes in the number of bites. It doesn't mean there's any fundamental change in marine ecosystems. It doesn't mean that a bunch of sharks have moved into your area. It might be nothing more than natural variability, which occurs in marine or terrestrial systems. Nature is an inherently noisy system. Part of the noise is variation in stuff, including the number of people that get bitten by sharks.

Across the Pacific in Australia, the number of people bitten by sharks has increased dramatically during the past two decades. It peaked in 2015, with 22 unprovoked shark attacks recorded by the Australian Shark Attack File, accounting for more than 22 per cent of the worldwide total. Discounting the US, there were more unprovoked shark attacks in Australia in 2015 than the rest of the world combined (there were eight attacks in South Africa, four on Réunion, two in the Canary Islands, two in the Galápagos Islands, with single incidents recorded in the Bahamas, Brazil, Egypt, New Caledonia and Thailand). Australia has a population of 24 million people. Its mainland has 35,000 kilometres of coastline, linked by 10,685 beaches. More than 85 per cent of Australians live within 50 kilometres of the coast and, thanks to the generally warm temperate climate, the beach is a place for leisure and pleasure. It is also an iconic, almost mythical space, integral to Australia's national identity and its famously laid-back, egalitarian lifestyle. The beach is seen by many as the great leveller of class, gender and race. The beach does not discriminate.

Neither does its marine life.

In 2015, there were unprovoked shark attacks on surfers, bodyboarders, swimmers, snorkellers, rowers, kayakers and surf ski paddlers. There were attacks on every corner of the continent: in New South Wales, Western Australia, Queensland, South Australia, Victoria and Tasmania. The grand total of 22 unprovoked attacks was almost double the ten-year average of 13. In fact, there were 14 attacks in northern New South Wales alone. There were also two fatal shark attacks, representing a third of the worldwide total: 41-year-old Tadashi Nakahara on 9 February 2015 and 46-year-old diver Damian Johnson, who died near Lachlan Island off Tasmania's east coast on 25 July 2015.

A 4.5-metre great white shark attacked Johnson while he was diving for scallops with his daughter in the Mercury Passage, about 2 kilometres off the Tasmanian coast and about 30 kilometres from a fur seal colony. The Tasmanian scallop season was closing in two days' time and, having assessed the morning's catch, the former professional urchin diver had gone back down for one final dive. When he did not resurface after 15 minutes, his daughter re-entered the water to look for him, only to find her father being attacked by a very large shark. It was the first fatal shark attack in Tasmanian waters in 22 years and was classified as a 'provoked encounter' – when a human purposely or accidentally attracts a shark through activities like fishing, spearfishing or cleaning fish – by John West, coordinator of the Australian Shark Attack File and manager of Life Sciences Operations at Taronga Zoo.

A stout man with a coarse grey beard, John West has been studying sharks for almost 50 years and is the oracle of the changing patterns of shark attacks in Australia, which have risen from an average of 6.5 unprovoked attacks a year between 1900 and 2000 to 15 unprovoked attacks a year over the next decade (2000 to 2010). He described the spike in shark attacks in Australia in 2015 as 'interesting', but like some maritime Methuselah he 'prefers to view trends over longer periods of time', for example decades, 'rather than trying to assign too much significance to year-to-year variability'. In 2015, he recorded 22 unprovoked and 11 provoked shark attacks in Australia. The raw numbers were almost 70 per cent higher than the average number of attacks recorded in the preceding three years, with a surprisingly high number (14) of unprovoked attacks occurring during the colder winter months (as opposed to eight attacks during summer). Great white sharks were responsible for 16 of the 22 unprovoked attacks, with 13 of those attacks involving surfers. This alarming trend continued in 2016. There were 26 recorded shark attacks in Australia in 2016, with 70% of all unprovoked attacks involving surfers.

Learn-to-surf schools have boomed in Australia during the past two decades: the number of accredited surf schools has risen from about 15 in the late 1990s to more than 100 in 2017. The country's peak surfing organisation, Surfing Australia, estimates that there are now more than 3 million surfers in Australia.

John West said that the sharp increase in the number of surfers during the past 25 years is largely responsible for the rising number of overall attacks. 'Surfing attacks increased by fifty per cent in the decade between 1995 and 2004 from the previous decade's figures. In 2005 to 2015 there was a further hundred and fifty per cent increase. Wetsuits have allowed people to spend more time in the water throughout the winter months. Most of the attacks by great white sharks occurred in the cooler months of the year on surfers.'

'Great white sharks are known to migrate long distances up and down the east and west coasts of Australia in the cooler months. [They] are very inquisitive and will investigate objects at the surface of the water, such as a surfboard, and these exploratory bites can be very serious to a human because of the size of the animals. I feel it was because of the combination of these events that northern New South Wales had the spike that was observed. The Western Australian cases from 2011 to 2013 [when there were 14 attacks, including six fatalities, in the space of three years] seemed to have a similar pattern of great white shark involvement with surfers.'

George Burgess confirmed that surfers are at the biggest risk of shark attack worldwide.

'Statistically, it's a Caucasian male between the ages of 14 and 28 who is surfing,' he told *Outside* magazine. 'As a group, around the world, surfers are the number one group. That's who is spending the most time in the water, where the sharks are most common, and doing things that are provocative. Surfing is a pro-vocative sport. There's a lot of kicking and arm splashing in the middle of an area where sharks are quite common. And surfers spend more time in the water than any other group. In Brazil, which didn't have a big history of shark attacks until the 1990s, suddenly things jumped up because surfing took off and you had more kids in the water.'

Numbers do not lie. John West said that, according to Australia's National Drowning Report, there had been an average of 292 drownings per year in Australia during the past decade.

'If anyone is to worry about anything when in the water, it should be about drowning rather than a shark attack,' he said.

George Burgess said that the rising number of shark attacks is directly related to human population growth, which amounts to around 75 million (or 1.13 per cent) more people on the planet each year.

'The shark attack *rate* is not increasing even though the number of shark attacks is rising,' he explained.

Consequently, he suggested that the number of people that get bitten by sharks would continue to increase into the future.

'Each year we should have more attacks than the previous year owing to the rise of human population from year to year.'

It's a neat explanation, but one that seems simplistic and difficult to swallow in so-called 'shark hot spots': places that have experienced a sudden, seemingly senseless frenzy of attacks, like Réunion Island, where there were 19 unprovoked shark attacks and seven fatalities in the six years from 2011 to 2016, followed by a further two fatal attacks in early 2017.

7

LA CRISE REQUIN

HE WAS 13 years old and small for his age, with a mop of sun-bleached hair, blue eyes and a honey-brown surfer tan. His parents called him Titi, which was French slang for a smart and spirited young boy, derived from a long-forgotten nineteenth-century Parisian phrase used to describe a new apprentice. It was Sunday morning on 12 April 2015, and the boy was walking a friend home along the coastal road of Rue des Sables, past the rocky headland of Cap Homard and the tourist resorts strung out along Réunion's picturesque west coast. They stopped at Les Aigrettes, a sandy beach littered with clumps of dead coral, where a small group of surfers danced across sapphire-blue waves in the tropical sunshine. Titi was transfixed.

Surfing and swimming had been banned on Réunion for almost two years, ever since French teenager Sarah Roperth was bitten in half while snorkelling 5 metres from shore in the Bay of Saint-Paul, less than 20 kilometres north of Les Aigrettes, on 15 July 2013. The 15-year-old girl's death marked the fifth fatal shark attack on Réunion in the space of two years. The unprecedented outbreak of attacks coincided with what scientists from France's Institute of Research Development (IRD) described as 'an imbalance, an abnormally high presence of particularly aggressive large sharks in the infested waters off the west coast of Réunion'. Most Réunion surfers were marooned on shore in the grip of fear, having lost friends, loved ones and limbs to *la crise requin* (the shark crisis). A handful of patrolled beaches had remained open, like the shallow lagoon at L'Hermitage, while surfers at more popular, seemingly 'safer' spots sometimes employed *vigies requin* (shark lookouts): small diving teams, armed with whistles and spear guns, that floated below the surface on the edge of the surf zone.

But this was different and Titi knew it. These were surfers, wild and brave and crazy, intoxicated by the pure freedom of the beautiful dance of man against Mother Nature.

Titi rushed home, left a note for his mum, and went surfing.

'Don't worry,' he wrote. 'If there's no security, I won't surf.'

But there were no lifeguards or shark lookouts at Les Aigrettes on that tranquil Sunday morning. There were just waves: flaw-lessly shaped left-handers coursing down the shallow coral reef, with half a dozen surfers swooping and looping through the line-up. Titi surfed for an hour and a half. He rode wave after wonderful wave, sating his ravenous, pent-up hunger. He finished his last ride, kicking off as the wave collapsed in the shallows, and struck out into the channel, paddling slower now, with tired arms and aching shoulders. The boy was suddenly flung up into the air, his torso trapped in the jaws of a large shark as it charged from below and viciously rag-dolled his body in a spreading pool of blood. The shark briefly let go before tearing at Titi's limbs, biting off his right arm and right leg, and then dragging his limp body out to sea.

'Titi was devoured by his passion,' his father Giovanni Canestri told French broadcaster RTL. 'He never went surfing alone, except the day it happened, unfortunately. [Titi and his friend] saw that the waves were amazing and that adults were surfing in the water. And by seeing adults in the water, he must have thought it was safe. There are no words to describe what must have happened. He got attacked twice, so he had time to realise what was happening to him. And that is hard … Fate decided one day to take him away and he is gone.'

Réunion is a volcanic outcrop that rises spectacularly out of the Indian Ocean in the middle of nowhere, about 2000 kilometres from the African mainland, east of Madagascar and south-west of Mauritius. Historically a wild, dangerous place haunted by pirates, convicts and slave traders, Réunion has morphed into a popular tourist destination, marketed as 'the intense island' for its dramatic volcanoes, exotic wildlife and coral-fringed coastline. Réunion has a permanent population of less than 850,000 people and a coastline of just 207 kilometres. Yet the horrific death of 13-year-old junior surfing champion Elio 'Titi' Canestri was the eighteenth unprovoked shark attack and seventh fatality recorded off the coast of Réunion in the space of just four years, from 2011 to 2015. The frenzy of attacks made international headlines, with Réunion referred to simply as 'Shark Island', while two of the six fatalities the International Shark Attack File (ISAF) recorded in 2015 occurred on this tiny French territory.

For such a small island, Réunion has an oversized reputation for sharks. Réunion's marine observatory recorded 30 attacks and 17 fatalities from 1972 to 2011. However, the dramatic spike in shark activity that began in 2011 was uncharted territory, as frightening as it was complex. Marine biologists suggested that the island's climate and geography were perfectly suited for sharks, particularly the bull shark, the prime suspect in almost every attack. The volcanic island has steep slopes, with Piton de la Fournaise (Peak of the Furnace), an active volcano on the eastern end of the island, rising 2632 metres above sea level. Although the coastline is surrounded by coral reefs, like Hawaii Réunion has no continental shelf, so the ocean floor drops abruptly into deep water, bringing large marine animals close to shore. Its wet season is six months of the year, from November to April, and Réunion holds world records for the most rainfall in 12-, 24-, 72- and 96-hour periods. Heavy rains wash plumes of muddy water out into the ocean, providing the preferred conditions for bull sharks to scavenge for food.

These naturally occurring conditions have collided with some unnatural ones. Réunion has experienced rapid population growth. The island's population grew by 9 per cent between 1999 and 2006. There was increased tourism, with visitor numbers rising by almost 70 per cent between 2006 and 2011. The island's sewerage and drainage basins became overloaded, adding waste-water and effluent to the run-off from rain. Coastal development and deforestation caused erosion of the island's steep slopes, further muddying the waters.

There was documented evidence of overfishing by longliners, which some conservationists suggested had devastated the sharks' natural food supply. Professional shark fishing had stopped. French authorities introduced regulations in 1999 that banned the consumption of several shark species, including tiger and bull sharks, because of the risk of food poisoning from marine biotoxins, especially ciguatoxins (188 people were admitted to hospital with food poisoning in Madagascar in November 1993 after eating the meat from a single bull shark, resulting in 98 deaths). International shark finning regulations were introduced in 2004, requiring fishermen to retain the entire shark carcass (fins could not weigh more than 5 per cent of the total catch), forcing the remaining shark fishermen on Réunion out of business.

A controversial marine nature reserve was established along a 19-kilometre stretch of the island's west coast in 2007 to restore depleted fish stock and protect Réunion's fragile coral reef. A decade-long French Institute of Research Development (IRD) study found that marine biodiversity had rapidly declined and the reef had been significantly degraded by high visitor pressure and pollution. However, local surfers and tourist operators accused the marine scientists of turning the island's west coast into an 'ecological experiment' and creating a 'larder' for sharks close to shore. Project manager of Réunion's Regional Fisheries Committee, marine biologist David Guyomard, told UK newspaper *The Daily Telegraph* that there was an 'overpopulation' problem with bull sharks in the area.

'It's wrong to describe it as an infestation – there aren't hundreds of thousands of them,' said Guyomard, who co-authored a study on the seasonal variability of bull and tiger sharks on the island's west coast. 'But it is fair to say that we have a problem.'

The bull shark (*Carcharhinus leucas*) is named for its short, blunt snout as well as its pugnacious temperament and tendency to headbutt prey before biting. It can grow to up to 4 metres in length and its body is round and stout with a large dorsal fin. It is capable of short, powerful bursts of speed. Also known as the Zambezi or Nicaragua shark, on Réunion it is referred to as *le bouledogue* (the bulldog). Notoriously aggressive, it is also regarded as one of the most intelligent shark species: behavioural studies in the US found that bull sharks could discriminate between different colours and used visual cues to differentiate between objects. However, its very small eyes and tendency to attack in turbid water suggest that eyesight is not a particularly important hunting tool.

The bull shark has a predilection for warm, shallow water but is highly adaptive and can swim in both salt water and fresh water through a process called osmoregulation, which is incredibly complicated to explain but essentially results in the bull shark peeing about 20 times more in fresh water than they do in salt water.

Bull sharks were responsible for two fatal attacks in the space of 96 days at Réunion's most popular tourist beach in 2011, sparking *la crise requin*. Boucan Canot is an idyllic slice of tropical paradise near the busy tourist resorts of Saint-Gilles. But on 15 June 2011, several bull sharks attacked 31-year-old local bodyboarder Eddy Auber at Boucan Canot, biting off his right arm and savagely mauling his body. It was viewed as an isolated, tragic incident, until French bodyboarding champion Mathieu Schiller was attacked at the very same beach on 19 September 2011.

Schiller had operated a surf school at Boucan Canot since 2008. The day's final class had cleared the water about 45 minutes before he paddled out to catch a late afternoon wave, despite lifeguards having raised an orange 'shark flag' warning people to stay out of the ocean. As soon as Schiller reached the deep water beyond the breaking waves, where a group of half a dozen surfers bobbed up and down in the large surf, the 32-year-old was attacked with 'terrifying speed' by at least two large bull sharks, possibly more.

He was unconscious and bleeding heavily from gaping wounds to his legs and torso when lifeguard and childhood friend Vincent Rzepecki reached him and managed to drag his body onto a rescue paddleboard. But the waves were too big and the current was too strong. Relentless walls of whitewater bashed into Rzepecki. He lost Schiller's body in the turbulence and almost drowned himself. Other lifeguards followed in a dinghy, only to be charged by a very large, highly agitated bull shark, estimated to be 4 metres long. Schiller's body was never recovered.

Boucan Canot rose with the speed of a bullet in online lists of the world's most dangerous beaches. There had not been a single shark attack on Réunion in 2010. Suddenly there was a dramatic spike in shark activity, centred on a 30-kilometre stretch of surf-kissed coastline in the Saint-Paul district, with most incidents occurring within the marine nature reserve. It began on 19 February 2011, four months before Eddy Auber was killed, when a bull shark attacked French surfer Eric Dargent at Trois Roches, a few kilometres south of Boucan Canot, tearing off his left leg just above the knee. There had been heavy rain on Réunion and several shark sightings at the nearby Saint-Gilles harbour. Fatefully, it was Mathieu Schiller who highlighted the heightened danger.

'With the dirty water pouring through the ravines, it is known that the risk is multiplied,' Schiller told *Le Journal de l'île de*

La Réunion. 'However, we must not demonise. It is more likely to have an accident than be attacked by a shark.'

On 13 October 2011, less than a month after Schiller was killed, the 'partly devoured' body of an unidentified woman was found floating near shore at La Possession, around 12 kilometres north of Boucan Canot. Authorities retrieved a leg and torso pocked with bite marks and, although an autopsy a few days later confirmed the probable cause of death as shark attack, it was not included in ISAF's official statistics.

However, ISAF investigated a record number of shark attacks on Réunion in 2011. On 6 July 2011, a few weeks after Auber's fatal attack, a bull shark charged 16-year-old local surfer Arnaud Dussel at nearby Les Roches Noires beach, biting a large chunk out of his surfboard. On 5 October 2011, a shark bit 51-year-old Jean-Pierre Castellani's outrigger canoe in half near Cape la Houssaye, a few kilometres north of Boucan Canot. Castellani bashed the shark on the head with his paddle before capsizing and spending 10 terrifying minutes floating helplessly in the water.

'I completely freaked out,' Castellani confessed to *Le Journal de l'île de La Réunion.* 'In three seconds [the shark] bit twice and the canoe is left as the matchstick. Once in the water, I thought he was going to come back and I would die.'

A passing boat rescued Castellani, who vowed to 'never set a foot in the water' again. Local diver Jean-Paul Delaunay perhaps wished he had followed that advice. On 11 November 2011, he had his left foot bitten off by a bull shark while spearfishing at Saint-Rose, on the island's east coast.

The deadly trend continued in 2012. On 23 July 2012, a bull shark attacked local surfer Alexandre Rassiga at Trois-Bassins, one of the island's most popular surf spots, a few kilometres south of Boucan Canot. The shark tore off the 21-year-old bartender's leg, severing his femoral artery, and he bled to death on the beach. Rassiga's death sparked angry protests from local surfers, who marched on Réunion's capital, Saint-Denis, calling for the marine reserve to be immediately opened to shark fishing.

'We are fed up with hearing scientists say that the reserve can't be the only reason for this proliferation and for these attacks,' Ludovic Villedieu from Réunion's Radical Surf Club told French broadcaster Euronews.

On 5 August 2012, a bull shark attacked prominent local surfer Fabien Bujon at the island's most famous surf break, Saint-Leu, biting off his right hand and lower leg. While Bujon miraculously survived the violent encounter, rage boiled over and an angry mob attacked the marine reserve office. Mayor of Saint-Leu, Thierry Robert MP, responded by authorising the hunting of bull sharks 'by any means' and promising to pay €2 per kilo for the first 30 sharks caught. (An adult bull shark can weigh as much as 300 kilograms.) The decree was met with howls of indignation from French conservation groups, led by sex siren–cum–animal rights activist Brigitte Bardot, who wrote a letter to French prime minister Jean-Marc Ayrault, labelling the decision 'blind'.

'We can't condemn sharks to death just to please surfers. It's ridiculous.'

French authorities intervened and the mayor was forced to withdraw the order two days later, as it contravened French conservation laws regarding fishing in marine reserves.

The attacks continued, each one seemingly more horrific and grotesque than the last. On 8 May 2013, a bull shark attacked French tourist Stéphane Berhamel at Brisant beach, a few hundred metres south of Trois-Bassins, on the opposite side of the mouth of the Ravine Saint-Gilles. The shark charged the 36-year-old twice before fatally biting his thigh. Berhamel and his wife were honeymooning on Réunion. His wife was sunbathing on the beach during the attack. The couple had an 18-month-old daughter.

Then, on 15 July 2013, 15-year-old Sarah Roperth was sliced in half 5 metres from shore in the bay of Saint-Paul. Two bull sharks were caught in the vicinity within 72 hours of the attack, but the lower half of the teenager's body was never recovered. Local authorities responded by banning surfing and swimming at unsupervised beaches, which covered about 90 per cent of the Réunion coast. Sixteen of the island's 17 surf schools were forced to close. The remaining school provided stand-up paddleboard lessons in L'Hermitage lagoon.

David Guyomard's team of scientists at the Regional Fisheries Committee had tagged 45 tiger sharks and 38 bull sharks to study behaviour and movement patterns. But the scientific approach was slow, and patience was in short supply. Consequently, authorities gained approval from France's Directorate General for Food to 'cull' 90 sharks (45 tiger sharks and 45 bull sharks), ostensibly to analyse the level of ciguatoxins and heavy metals (lead, cadmium and mercury) found in their bodies. This time, the complaints from conservation groups fell on deaf ears.

Shark activity momentarily slowed. The islanders thought that the cull had solved the 'shark problem' and that man had conquered Mother Nature, ending the devastating *crise requin*. There was just one solitary shark attack on Réunion in 2014: a juvenile tiger shark charged 51-year-old surfer Vincent Rintz at Saint-Leu, biting his calf and wrist. Rintz survived the attack with minor lacerations. But the relief was short-lived. On 14 February 2015, Valentine's Day, 22-year-old British tourist Talon Bishop was swimming in waist-deep water with her boyfriend at the beach at L'Étang-Salé (the Salty Pond), south of Saint-Leu, when a tiger shark bit her leg and dragged her underwater. She was rushed to Holy Land Hospital at Saint-Pierre but was pronounced dead on arrival. Then, on 12 April 2015, Elio 'Titi' Canestri was attacked at Les Aigrettes. More than a thousand people attended a memorial for Titi, with his father, Giovanni, leading a protest march to Saint-Denis, where he tipped red paint on the street and demanded action from authorities.

'I have two children left and I want them to stay alive,' Giovanni told Agence France-Presse (AFP).

Ludovic Villedieu did not attend Titi's memorial or the subsequent protest. Instead, Ludovic spent the day building a makeshift shark barrier with garden hoses and fishing buoys, which was then chained to the ocean floor at Boucan Canot.

After enduring four years of fear and terror, Réunion's surfing community began fighting back to reclaim the ocean. Patrick Flores, father of professional surfer Jeremy Flores, was elected deputy mayor of Saint-Paul district and immediately began agitating to implement a multifaceted shark mitigation strategy. The tourism industry, reeling from a 30 per cent drop in visitor numbers, lobbied the French government for funding.

'The shark crisis hit our economy hard,' Chairman of Réunion Island Tourism Stéphane Fouassin lamented in the documentary *Surrounded: Island of the Sharks*. 'The entire world was talking about Réunion Island and its risk of shark attacks. Entire industries have been destroyed – victims of a natural disaster.'

In February 2016, a 610-metre shark net was installed at Boucan Canot and a 500-metre net was installed at Les Roches Noires. The mesh nets were chained to the ocean floor, up to 11 metres below the surface. So-called 'smart' drum lines (baited hooks attached to buoys with GPS devices to alert fishermen when a shark was hooked) were also positioned along Réunion's west coast. Large bull and tiger sharks caught by the drum lines were killed, while smaller sharks and other marine life were released.

'I think their idea of smart drum lines is a really good one,' shark expert Geremy Cliff from South Africa's KwaZulu-Natal Sharks Board told *The Daily Telegraph*. 'But I recommended that they start properly fishing again, too – even in the face of opposition from conservationists. I'm sceptical that this story of bacterial infections in the sharks is really reason to prevent commercial fishing. You can't just sit back and say don't go in the water. It's gone too far on Réunion.'

There was a single unprovoked attack in 2016. 21-year-old surfer Laurent Chardard had his arm and foot bitten off by a bull shark at Boucan Canot in August. The beach was closed at the time after a two-metre hole had been discovered in the shark net. Then nothing for six months. Just when you thought it was safe to go back in the water, bodyboarders Alexandre Naussac and Adrien Dubosc were killed in almost identical circumstances in the space of two months in early 2017: both were bitten on the thigh by a bull shark, severing the femoral artery, while surfing in shallow, murky water. Surfing legend Kelly Slater took to Twitter to call for a 'serious cull on Réunion, and it should happen every day'.

There is a clear imbalance happening in the ocean there. If the whole world had these rates of attack nobody would use the ocean and […] millions of people would be dying like this.

Weather-beaten Australian expatriate Mick Asprey has been surfing the sapphire-blue waves in the tropical sunshine of Réunion for more than 40 years. Ruddy-faced with a halo of white fluffy hair and one bung eye, blinded by a surfboard that boomeranged back into his face a decade ago, the 68-year-old arrived on Réunion in 1975 aboard a freighter from Madagascar 'full of pigs, goats and zebus'. He hitchhiked around the island and stumbled across the small notch in the reef at Saint-Leu where perfect, mesmerising left-handers wrapped into a pretty lagoon. Mick was transfixed. He said later that he felt like he'd 'found a treasure'.

'When you find a treasure, you don't tell anyone,' he explained.

Armed with a pharmacy degree from Sydney University, Mick started making surfboards instead, trading seasons between Jeffreys Bay in South Africa and Saint-Leu on Réunion. In 1987, he established his Mickey Rat surf shop and surfboard factory on a hill overlooking the famous surf break.

'I don't think there were attacks around that time, before the 1990s – there probably weren't enough people in the water.'

Réunion is different now: more populated, more tourists and more shark attacks. Mick described the situation as 'disastrous' for his small island home.

'Everyone who gets taken, bitten or eaten is someone everyone knows, [because] everybody knows everybody.'

He said that allowing fishermen to fish for sharks again 'could help to reduce numbers and balance things out a bit' but suggested a more ruthless approach was required.

'If they had that rate of attacks on Sydney beaches they'd kill all the sharks. I don't have a problem with it, especially when they are killing your friends.'

8

FISH ARE FRIENDS

THE LITTLE GIRL floated gently out into the big blue. Strands of her long dark hair swayed in the water. Behind the glass of a dive mask, her big brown eyes widened as she drifted further into the otherworld under the sea, among the coral, anemones and brightly coloured damselfish. She floated further out, off the edge of Julian Rocks, an ancient, metamorphic outcrop beyond the easternmost point of the Australian mainland. Her eyes darted from side to side, searching, not for green turtles or pretty vermilion sea stars or even bright-yellow angelfish. The young girl was looking for sharks – the endangered grey nurse shark (*Carcharias taurus*) to be precise, which frequented Julian Rocks and the Cape Byron Marine Park during the winter months to breed. Suddenly two large white-bellied creatures appeared, gliding slowly along the bottom. With their sharp, pointy snouts, beady eyes and long, narrow teeth, they looked fearsome.

But the girl was not afraid – quite the opposite. It was her twelfth birthday. And all her dreams had just come true.

That little girl was Madison Stewart, better known as 'Shark Girl', the name of the 2014 documentary about her fight to protect sharks on Australia's Great Barrier Reef.

'It was a really amazing, humbling experience,' the now 23-year-old said, reflecting on that pre-teen encounter off Byron Bay more than a decade ago. 'Nothing prepares you for it. No matter how much you see them on TV, it is always different in real life. I'd never seen anything so perfectly adapted to its environment. I can still picture it to this day and I think it will stick with me forever. It was just a really beautiful and fascinating moment for me.'

Madison Stewart was captivated by sharks from a young age. She lived aboard a yacht on the Great Barrier Reef for the first few years of her life. Her dad, Ernst, had turned his back on a career as a university lecturer in physiology to become an accredited PADI (Professional Association of Diving Instructors) divemaster, and Madi spent a lot of time in the ocean as a baby.

'We'd find little bays where Madi could swim with sea creatures,' Ernst recalled in *Shark Girl*.

By the age of seven, Madi was obsessed with the underwater world, swimming, snorkelling and watching nature documentaries with her dad.

'My childhood obsession was the Great Barrier Reef,' she explained in *Shark Girl*. 'I remember schools of fish that would block out the sun, coral rising up from the darkness. I remember sharks. I love sharks. I have never felt fear of them.'

Madi referred to the Great Barrier Reef as 'my Disneyland' and sharks as 'my family'.

'I love sharks like my siblings. It's like messing around with the little brother or the little sister that I never had.'

She dreamed of diving with sharks like her dad, but the minimum age for certification as a scuba diver in Australia was 12 years old. (It has since been raised to 14.)

'She was marking off the days on her calendar,' Ernst said in *Shark Girl*. 'She only had five years to mark off. She couldn't wait.'

That first dive off Julian Rocks on her twelfth birthday changed Madi's life, reinforcing her deep fascination with sharks. 'I think it's absolutely in our instinct and in our DNA to be fascinated with predators. I think everyone has that fascination but some people embrace it more. A lot of people love cute and fluffy animals, but certain people really bond with animals like sharks. It's not because we see them as cute and fluffy, but I think we embrace them for what they are. When you are a kid and you are on a dive boat, everybody is dying to see a turtle. When you mention sharks there is a different reaction. I love that. I respect that. I think that was something that really attracted me to them – the *Jaws* factor. I like that about them, that they actually spark fear in people. I have always been different and I've always been attracted to monsters and wanted to be on the side of the underdog.'

Madi thinks sharks are the ultimate underdogs: misunderstood by the public, miscast by the media and persecuted by governments and commercial fisheries, which were decimating shark populations on her beloved Great Barrier Reef. 'When I was fourteen, I went back to one of the places on the Great Barrier Reef that I had been diving before, but much to my surprise there were no sharks there anymore. At a really young age, I had witnessed the collapse of a population, and that's when I turned into a conservationist. The sharks I knew and loved and grew up with had been stripped from the reef and reduced to a mere few at the hands of unjustified harvesting inside the marine park by commercial gillnet vessels approved by the Australian government. I learnt very quickly how easily change can occur and how conservation was not an option for me, but a necessity and an obligation to the creatures and the oceans I love. But to be a child who wants to make a difference is not easy, and I needed a way to be heard. This is when I started to make films.'

At the tender age of 14, Madi convinced her dad to let her leave elite Gold Coast girls' boarding school St Hilda's to be home schooled, using the money saved on school fees to buy underwater camera equipment. 'Most girls my age spent their time at the mall or talking about boys. I chased sharks with my dad. I didn't fit in. Leaving school was the best thing that ever happened to me. I knew what I was passionate about. Leaving school helped it happen. [But] my grandmother was the first one to absolutely panic. She's never been big on the whole 'diving with sharks' thing.'

Thus, Madi's award-winning filmmaking career began, despite her grandmother's reservations. She swam with bull, great white, grey nurse, hammerhead, lemon, tiger and whitetip reef sharks. She travelled to shark sanctuaries in the Bahamas and Palau. She learned how to induce tonic immobility in reef sharks by stroking them under the snout and sending them into a natural paralysis. She became Shark Girl. 'Tiger sharks are my favourites. They are described as the great whites of the tropics. They're big. They're beautiful. You feel their presence. They're the shark that you know that you don't mess with. I really love them for that.'

She built up a library of incredible footage of close encounters and began editing short films on iMovie, uploading them to YouTube and screening them at film festivals. She was convinced that if people could see how beautiful sharks were in their natural environment and better understand their importance to the marine ecosystem of the Great Barrier Reef, it would change public perception.

'The irrational fear humans have of sharks is contributing to the demise of ninety per cent of the world's sharks,' she explained. 'This wouldn't be happening if they were dolphins or whales. People don't want to fight for sharks because they're scared of them. So I started making films to show people what was happening with sharks to get them to have a different opinion. Sharks need a voice more than any other animal; they are the unsung and misrepresented heroes of our oceans. I am actually unsure if they will have a place in my future after what I have seen, and that terrifies me. So many people see them as a bloodthirsty mindless killer, but I see them as totally misunderstood. The only thing scary about sharks is what we, the human race, have done to them. My mission in life is to do everything in my power to protect them. The main focus of my mission is to end the legal shark fisheries inside the Great Barrier Reef. It is unnecessary and unjust, and I want to see it come to an end. I just hope I can persuade people that sharks aren't mindless killers and that they're a vital part of the ocean.'

Marine ecosystems are complex and tightly interwoven.

'From all of the evidence we have, these large predators are vitally important to healthy ecosystems, which is probably why sharks have been around for 450 million years,' Professor Jessica Meeuwig, director of the Centre for Marine Futures at the University of Western Australia, explained. 'We have clear evidence from land that the big predators like wolves and lions are absolutely fundamental in maintaining ecosystem health. For instance, when wolves were eliminated from Rùm Island off Scotland the red deer went nuts and the forest died from overgrazing.

'We are starting to see the same pattern in the ocean, that when you remove sharks it has a negative impact on the reefs themselves. Tiger sharks have been implicated in maintaining healthy sea grass communities, which relates to climate change. You remove the tiger sharks, the turtles and other herbivores go nuts, and that has negative impacts on sea grass communities which are critically important to storage of carbon.'

The suggested link to climate change underlines how everything in the marine ecosystem is interconnected. There is compelling scientific evidence from the United Nations Inter-governmental Panel on Climate Change (IPCC) that climate change is harming the rich biodiversity of the Great Barrier Reef. Extensive aerial and underwater surveys conducted by the Australian Research Council Centre for Coral Reef Studies at James Cook University in 2016 revealed that coral bleaching had affected 93 per cent of the reef. An Australian Institute of Marine Science study found that the Great Barrier Reef had lost around 50 per cent of its coral cover between 1985 and 2012. The Coral Sea has recorded significant increases in sea surface temperatures during that period, with March 2016 being the warmest month on record.

'The Great Barrier Reef is in grave danger,' Sir David Attenborough declared in his 2015 documentary *David Attenborough's Great Barrier Reef*. 'The twin perils brought by climate change – an increase in the temperature of the ocean and in its acidity – threaten its very existence.'

In turn, Madi has argued that a certain fishery threatens the existence of sharks on the Great Barrier Reef. The Queensland East Coast Inshore Fin Fish Fishery is a commercial gillnet fishery that operates within the marine park and, since 1994, has increasingly targeted sharks to meet the growing demand for shark fins from lucrative Asian markets (where fins can sell for as much as $500 per kilogram), while the meat sells as 'flake', a conveniently ambiguous staple of local fish and chip shops across Australia.

> According to a report by the Great Barrier Reef Marine Park Authority: The pressure on sharks in the Great Barrier Reef increased between 1990 and 2003, with more specialist shark fishers entering the gillnet fishery and more effort being directed at targeting sharks.
>
> Commercial fishery logbooks have recorded a significant increase in reported shark catch and effort in the net fishery in the Great Barrier Reef, rising from 295 tonnes from 191 boats in 1994 and peaking at 1202 tonnes from 221 boats in 2003.

A rezoning of the marine park resulted in the buyout of 59 net licenses in 2006 and the Queensland government implemented a 600 tonne Total Allowable Catch (TAC) quota for the fishery in 2009. However, Madi said that around 80 per cent of the total quota (about 480 tonnes) was taken from within the Great Barrier Reef Marine Park, a World Heritage Area, and included species that are classified as 'near threatened', 'vulnerable', 'endangered' and 'critically endangered'.

'There is no such thing as a sustainable shark fishery based on an already suffering population of sharks,' she said. 'Sharks are basically a non-renewable resource because they are slow growing, mature late and have few offspring, and are therefore highly susceptible to fishing pressure. All the evidence is right in front of us – this fishery should not exist. We are putting every other fishery around it at risk by allowing the targeting of an apex predator, causing a cascade effect in the ecosystem they control. Not to mention the countless jobs in the tourism industry.'

Tourism on the Great Barrier Reef contributed $5.68 billion to the Australian economy and generated almost 70,000 full-time jobs, according to a 2013 study by Deloitte Access Economics. Tourist numbers surged following the release of Disney's 2003 animated blockbuster *Finding Nemo*, which was used in Tourism Australia marketing campaigns in China and the United States. Despite the film's conservation message, *Finding Nemo* was both a blessing and a curse for the reef. The sudden rise in tourist numbers placed increased pressure on the fragile ecosystem, while the spike in demand for clownfish from aquariums and pet shops pushed the already threatened species to the brink of extinction. (The Saving Nemo Conservation Fund has since been created to breed clownfish in captivity to take pressure off wild stocks and provide education about 'ornamental' marine species.) But alongside Nemo, Dory and Marlin, one of the surprise stars of the film was a great white shark called Bruce, voiced by Australian satirist Barry Humphries.

'I am a nice shark, not a mindless eating machine,' Bruce declared in his Fish-Friendly Shark Pledge. 'If I am to change this image, I must first change myself. Fish are friends, not food.'

'I thought that was awesome,' Madi said. 'It was cool to see sharks represented that way in a movie. They usually get a bad rap. I think it was very brave of them to do that – to not to make them the enemy for once. What was really cool was how it resonated with young people. I think it showed that we'd moved on from the *Jaws* generation, that sharks are [seen as] more than just bloodthirsty killers.'

Despite her love for them, Madi does not pretend that sharks do not kill people.

'They're big, dangerous animals,' she said. 'We need to embrace them as a dangerous and ever-present part of our coastline. We cannot hate or exterminate a creature operating in its own home, [doing] what it is meant to do, but we can arm ourselves with the best knowledge possible.'

She has interviewed Vic Hislop and discussed the famous shark hunter's theory about killing large dangerous sharks to help 'Mother Nature keep a balance'.

'He's not wrong about everything but he is wrong about how the food chain works,' said Madi. 'He has a very basic and incorrect understanding of a shark's place in the ocean. The idea that we need to thin things out to create a balance does not work when you're talking about apex predators at the top of the food chain. They are already in small numbers because of the food chain triangle. They actually control the populations below them. People like Vic – they represent the past. He is more of a verbal threat to sharks through spreading misinformation than the commercial fisheries, which are wiping out sharks. But it's definitely a great thing that his museum has shut down. It was archaic ten years ago.'

Madi said that she understands the emotional response to fatal shark attacks, but that grief and fear should not be manipulated to justify hunting and killing sharks. 'My first feeling is sadness for that person and that person's family and friends, as well as anyone who witnessed what happened. It's horrific and really heartbreaking. My second feeling is anger that something probably could've been done to prevent it. [Then] it makes me anxious because I know the next thing that's going to come is the media pandemonium and people starting to freak out wanting sharks killed. But it can no longer be an emotional response. That's when facts get pushed aside and things get twisted. Politicians thrive in the blood of shark attack victims. So do commercial fishermen, so do fisheries, and so does the media – especially the media – and I hate the idea of people using other people's tragic deaths as a way to boost their occupation.'

Madi said that surfers (who accounted for 68 per cent of all unprovoked shark attacks in Australia in 2015) should take more responsibility for putting themselves in dangerous situations and acknowledge the impact that the consequent attacks had upon the wider community.

A self-confessed 'terrible longboarder', Madi said that swimming with sharks was a very different proposition to floating on the surface with a surfboard. 'I'm scared when I'm on a surfboard. It's a completely different thing. Surfers are on the frontline of shark interactions; they're in the most dangerous spots at the most dangerous times. I absolutely understand the addictive nature of surfing. I've done my research. I've dated a few surfers. The real surfers have the mentality that it's [the sharks'] territory and whatever happens, happens. But I think that it's absolutely necessary that people find ways to protect themselves in the ocean. There is an increasing gap between fear and understanding. Shark safety is not spoken about in schools. It's not part of the curriculum when we learn about currents and rips and tides. Kids don't learn about the risk of swimming at dusk and dawn, around bait balls, in murky water. We're in total denial about this animal's presence. That's why it's so frustrating to see people go out and surf in the middle of a huge bait ball, or at dusk. They need to think about the repercussions, not only on their own lives, but the whole community, if and when they get attacked. Because it's fear that is motivating things like culling and shark nets. They're futile activities. Education is a way to help prevent dangerous situations with sharks, not killing them.'

When the Western Australian government introduced its controversial drum line policy in January 2014, aimed at capturing and killing large sharks in the vicinity of swimming beaches with baited hooks, Madi joined marine conservation organisations Sea Shepherd and Animal Amnesty in Western Australia to follow, observe and document the so-called 'shark cull'.

The controversial policy was developed in reaction to a spate of seven shark-related deaths in Western Australian waters in the space of four years, from 2010 to 2013. But it was not universally popular. More than 6000 people rallied at Perth's Cottesloe Beach amid nationwide protests after the second shark, a 2-metre tiger shark, was killed off Leighton Beach in North Fremantle on 1 February 2014. A total of 172 sharks were caught during the 13-week trial, from January to April 2014. Sixty-eight of those sharks were shot and killed. Nearly all of the attacks in Western Australia from 2010 to 2013 were attributed to great whites, but the drum lines did not catch a single great white shark. Instead, Madi filmed tiger sharks caught on baited hooks. She filmed WA Fisheries officers shooting sharks with .22 calibre rifles.

She was involved in an ill-fated attempt to recover the carcass of a tiger shark being dumped at sea and was later questioned by WA Fisheries officers. She was filmed with her head pressed to the dead creature's nose, caught in inconsolable anguish, sobbing on the back of the Sea Shepherd dinghy.

The experience in Western Australia seemed to make Madi even more indignant with rage and righteous anger.

'Imagine being accused of being in possession of a protected species by the authorities that had just killed it,' she challenged in the narration of the subsequent short film, *Obstruction Is Justice*.

'The day we begin to back down in the face of injustice and not expose the negligence of the very people appointed to protect the animals they have now been hired to kill is the day we lose more than our sharks – we lose our ability to distinguish right from wrong.'

The emotive tone and breathless, husky voice-over of *Obstruction Is Justice*, far removed from the slickly produced, fact-based *Shark Girl*, would become Madi's trademark in short films like *Rise Up* and *My World*, decrying 'government scum' and depicting her at 'war' with the world.

'It is absolutely a war,' she said. 'It is a personal war for me because everything that I loved as a kid was taken away from me for profit by fisheries through mismanagement of our resources. That's what people call them – resources. I knew them as siblings and the most important thing to me was the interaction that I could have with sharks. It was so rare and that's what separated me from the crowd and made me feel special. But to other people they were simply resources and they were exploited and they have absolutely disappeared from some places [on the Great Barrier Reef]. I think there is a war going on, between people like myself and industry. The other war is the one that we are waging on the ocean, putting up fences and trying to make all our beaches shark proof. The funny thing about that war is that sharks don't even know they're involved in it.'

Experimental shark nets (essentially, cyclone wire fencing buoyed by huge steel drums) were introduced at Bondi Beach in March 1929 after two fatal attacks in the space of 28 days at the iconic Sydney beach. Nearby Coogee Beach followed suit and more widespread mesh netting was introduced to Sydney's metropolitan beaches in October 1937, as recommended by the NSW government's Shark Menace Advisory Committee, initially as a measure to prevent fatal shark attacks during the celebrations of 150 years of white settlement in 1938.

The committee held 44 meetings with local councils and surf clubs during a five-month consultation period, but the final recommendation of systematic and continuous netting at all beaches between Broken Bay and Port Hacking was met with ridicule by local authorities, including the president of the Royal Zoological Society, Theodore Cleveland Roughley. A marine zoologist who would later author *The Cult of the Goldfish* (1949), *Fish and Fisheries of Australia* (1957) and *Wonders of the Great Barrier Reef* (1961), Roughley suggested the proposal was 'futile' and 'would have practically no effect on the mathematical chances of surfers being attacked'.

'The area to be netted would be, in effect, a form of barrier, but the sharks could pass it at either end,' he explained to the committee.

However, with vocal support from the Surf Life Saving Association, 300-metre mesh nets were installed on 29 October

1937 about 400 metres offshore of Bondi, Bronte, Manly and North Steyne beaches at a cost of £20,000. Twenty-six sharks were caught during the first weekend of operation, as well as a porpoise, a lobster and 30 stingrays.

Shark nets have become increasingly controversial because of this bycatch – the 50-centimetre mesh holes also entangle turtles, dugongs, whales, dolphins, rays and other harmless species of sharks, such as the endangered grey nurse. Shark nets are now installed at 51 New South Wales beaches, spanning 200 kilometres of coastline. Since their introduction in 1937, not one fatal shark attack has been recorded at beaches where nets have been installed (although there has been a fatal attack on a netted beach in Queensland, where nets are used in combination with drum lines). However, a comprehensive analysis of 50 years of data from NSW and South Africa found that shark mitigation strategies like drum lines and shark nets in a localised area had no statistical impact on the number of attacks – that, statistically, shark nets 'do nothing' to stop attacks.

Deakin University's Dr Laurie Laurenson told the ABC's *Four Corners* program:

> The underlying assumption of the netting programs is that if you reduce the number of sharks, you will reduce the number of attacks. We could not demonstrate a statistically significant relationship between the density of the sharks and the number of attacks in the localised area around Sydney, where there have been historically large numbers of attacks and there have been large numbers of mitigation programs.

Dr Laurenson said that the four-year study found that there was a strong correlation between the number of attacks in an area and the number of *people*, but that there was 'no statistically demonstrable relationship' between the number of attacks and the number of sharks.

'It's just simply not there. I'm surprised that it's not there, but it's not there.'

Dr Laurenson suggested the lack of fatalities at netted beaches was actually because lifeguards patrolled them. 'If you look at how far medical intervention has come since the 1960s, [lifeguards] are very, very, very good at it. The reason there have been no fatalities is because of early responders having sufficient training, having the right equipment and knowing exactly what to do. They get there early. They get people to hospital quickly.'

On 29 September 2015, the New South Wales government gathered some of the world's top shark scientists, representatives from the Surf Life Saving Association and various conservation organisations at Taronga Zoo to discuss shark mitigation solutions to combat the recent spike in shark attacks on the northern New South Wales coast. A report commissioned by the NSW Department of Primary Industries explored various shark mitigation technologies, including large-scale barriers, chemical and electrical repellants, sonar systems and land-based observation. A month later, on 29 October 2015, the NSW government unveiled a five-year, $16 million shark strategy that combined the trialling of new technologies and aerial surveillance with research (including acoustic and satellite tagging). The strategy included the use of drones, in-water sonar to track shark movement and the development of a mobile phone application that could be used to track tagged sharks in real time, as well as a barrier net stretching across North Wall at Ballina.

'We don't cull sharks in New South Wales,' NSW Minister for Primary Industries Niall Blair proudly declared on ABC News.

'That's why we've gone for a look into some of the new technologies and other suites of measures we can implement and that's what this response is about. It's been led by our scientists.'

However, implementation of the NSW government's grand strategy stalled almost immediately, which frustrated scientists, conservation groups and the local surf community.

'The policy by most governments has been to pump millions of dollars into research and mitigation strategies,' Fred Pawle opined in *The Australian*.

Ocean users are now growing tired of both. More than a decade of research has yielded little useful and sometimes contradictory information, and mitigation strategies, such as the now postponed and almost certainly futile plan to install a barrier net across the beach at Ballina, northern NSW, are either expensive, impractical or seemingly ineffective.

'Personally, I think the government putting millions of dollars into shark mitigation is absolutely ridiculous,' Madi said. 'There are plenty of things that would be easier that the government could do right now. Why don't we have a shark warning system in place like they do in South Africa? People argue that shark nets save people from shark attacks, but they don't. There have been thirty-six bites at netted beaches since they've been in place. Any one of those could've turned into a fatality but they didn't, simply because they occurred at beaches where there are lifeguards on duty. A quicker response time can save people, yet nothing is being done and no money is being spent on having quicker and easier beach access for ambulances, or installing some kind of panic button at beaches.

'Education is absolutely the number one first thing that needs to happen. There's no time to wait for it. All the kids in Ballina still surf in the river mouth where a bull shark attack is very likely. They need some form of immediate education to understand the risks.'

PART THREE

PART THREE

9

SURFER PUNCHES SHARK

SURF FANS FROM Sydney to San Diego, São Paulo and beyond were glued to the live webcast from Jeffreys Bay in South Africa, watching a familiar figure float motionlessly on the horizon. Mick Fanning was instantly recognisable, with his curved spine, hunched shoulders bunched with muscle and square, blonde head. It also helped that Fanning's lucky number seven and his surname were spelled out across a pale-blue rash vest.

It was the final of the J-Bay Open and the three-time world champion's opponent, fellow Australian surfer Julian Wilson, had caught the first wave of the 40-minute decider. Mick puffed his cheeks, juggling air from side to side, turned to see where Julian had finished his wave and scratched the side of his face, like a chess master pondering his next move. Then a large fin punctured the ocean behind him and he was tossed into a maelstrom of splashing, kicking, fins and limbs. Mick gripped his surfboard tightly but the shark knocked him loose, slapping him into the water and dragging him under. A wave crested in the foreground and he disappeared from view. A wild, unspeakable image rushed up into the minds of the online voyeurs, of Fanning being eaten alive, as the seconds ticked slowly by.

1, 2 …

'Holy shit,' former world surfing champion Martin Potter exhaled involuntarily across the internet.

3, 4 …

The webcast cut to a wide angle with Mick still obscured by the waves breaking in the foreground.

5, 6 …

The beach announcer began yelling at the water patrol in his sharp South African accent: 'Get over to Mick Fanning immediately! Get over there immediately! Get there now!'

7, 8 …

On the other side of the planet, in her Tweed Heads lounge room on Australia's Gold Coast, Liz Osborne, Mick Fanning's mum, stood up and ran over to the television.

'I was absolutely terrified,' Liz told ABC News. 'I went over to the television almost as though I could pull him out of the television. I just wanted to save him but there was nothing I could do. I just could not believe what I was seeing. I was so scared. I was so overwhelmed. I just thought when that wave came that he was gone. I thought we'd lost him.'

In the water, less than 30 metres away, Julian Wilson froze with fear.

'I literally saw the whole thing pop up behind him,' Julian said at a press conference held at Sydney Airport when the two surfers arrived back in Australia. 'It was a lot bigger than him and I honestly froze … I was freaking out. I saw him start to get manhandled by the shark and saw him get knocked off his board. A wave popped up between us and I started paddling for him, fearing for his life … [He] was away from his board, the shark had bitten through his leg rope, and the board was fifteen to twenty metres away from him. I went into panic mode. He was a sitting duck now … I felt like I couldn't get to him in time.'

A rescue boat and two jetskis raced across the screen, sirens sounded and webcast commentator Joe Turpel found blandness amongst the mayhem.

'Fanning needing some assistance,' he said matter-of-factly. 'He's swimming in to the beach as we sound the horn to stop the final.'

But Mick Fanning wasn't swimming in to the beach. Mick's surfboard was floating away towards the horizon, and he was floating, too, with the worst kinds of thoughts rushing between his ears. 'I was swimming and I thought: "This thing is going to eat my legs, I've got to stop." I turned around and I was thinking: "Okay, am I going to fight this thing or am I going to die? One way or another, I'm dead, so I might as well go down with a fight." To have those thoughts and to make that decision – it is a very scary decision to make, when you're ready to die.'

Mick Fanning was not ready to die. Not on this day or any other. Mick was no stranger to death. In 1998, just two months after

Mick's seventeenth birthday, his older brother Sean was killed in a car accident on Australia's Gold Coast. Mick and Sean were the youngest of five siblings in a tight-knit Irish immigrant family.

'We called them the little ones,' Mick's mum, Liz Osborne, said. 'They were inseparable. He looked up to Sean all of the time. He was like a little puppy with a bigger dog. He just did everything Sean did. They did everything together.'

They shared a bedroom and shared a dream of one day becoming professional surfers, chasing perfect waves around the planet. Then, one dark August night, they went to a party. Mick walked home. Sean and mate Joel Green got a lift in the back of a station wagon, which hurtled through the Tweed Heads night, missed a roundabout, jumped a curb and crashed into a Norfolk pine. Sean and Joel were thrown from the vehicle and instantly killed. Mick was picked up by an unmarked police car and taken home to break the news to his mum. He did not leave his room for four days.

Surf filmmaker Peter Kirkhouse (a.k.a. PK) had been staying with the Fanning family. He took Mick aside.

'Take Sean's spirit in and keep it with you, because now it's yours,' PK said in *Surf for Your Life*. 'Take on his energy and use it.'

The deaths of Sean Fanning and Joel Green tore the Gold Coast surfing community apart. Mick plumbed the depths of heartache and grief, holed up in the bedroom he once shared with his much-loved older brother, while friends and family worried that the happy-go-lucky teenager they knew and loved would never re-emerge intact.

But the ocean brought him back. When he eventually surfaced, Mick sought solace amongst the swells, as he recounted in *Surf for Your Life*, a biography cum self-help manual Mick penned with surf journalist Tim Baker, 'feeling the comfort of the wind and sea spray in my face, and the pulse of the wave under my feet'. As he said in biopic surf film *Mick, Myself & Eugene*, 'He was my brother, but he was also my best mate. It was really hard to get over it. There's not a day that goes by where I don't think about Sean. I think about him when I wake up and the waves are pumping, or if it's a beautiful sunrise. I think about him then; how cool it would be to have him there. I think about him a lot.'

He also thinks about what PK said to him in the hours after Sean's death.

'I didn't really think about it at the time, but when I think back, it really has carried with me,' he explained in *Surf for Your Life*. 'A lot of the time I feel like he's with me when I travel and compete.'

As a teenager, Mick Fanning was a raw surfing talent. Blessed with an elastic body and innate ability to generate speed on a surfboard, he was something of a natural. From the age of 12, he ran with a pack of Australia's most exciting young surfers, the Cooly Kids, who earned their stripes surfing Coolangatta's grinding point breaks of Snapper Rocks, Greenmount and Kirra. By 16, Mick had signed a lucrative contract with surf company Rip Curl and was a poster boy for the next generation of Australian surfing. He was dubbed 'White Lightning' by the surf media but, despite his raw ability, Mick did not taste competitive success until after Sean's death. 'Sean was really driven to succeed as a pro surfer. I think that's where my work ethic came from. It wasn't until the next year that I started again and really decided what I was going to do – I was going to compete full-on, no mucking around.'

That next year, 1999, Mick won the world's two richest Pro Junior surfing competitions. Then, at just 18 years of age, he defeated some of Australian surfing's biggest names, including childhood hero Mark Occhilupo, to win an invitational at Sandon Point, on the south coast of New South Wales. It was an emotional day. It would have been Sean's twenty-first birthday and Mick won $21,000 in prize money.

'I speak to him all the time. If I'm out in a heat, I say: "Sean, send me a good one." And I feel like I'm doing it for him as well. We were going to do the [professional surfing] tour together before he died and I think we would've pushed each other so hard that we both would've been here. It was his dream to be a pro surfer and now I feel that his dream is also my dream. I feel that I'm surfing for both of us.'

Mick's magic carpet ride had begun. In 2001, he won the world's longest-running professional surfing competition, the Rip Curl Pro at Bells Beach, as an unseeded sponsor's wildcard. The skinny 19-year-old went on to top surfing's second tier World Qualifying Series and qualify for the elite World Championship Tour – a year-long circuit of the world's most spectacular and exotic wave locations that resembles some teenage surf punk's wet dream, travelling from Australia to Brazil, Fiji, Tahiti, South Africa, California, France, Portugal and Hawaii.

Among all these perfect waves, Mick formed a special connection with Jeffreys Bay. The freight-train right-hander felt like it was made for his super-fast surfing and Mick won the first competition he ever contested at the famous South African surf break, held in perfect 6- to 8-foot surf. It was the only win of his rookie year on tour. He was joined on the podium by a group of kids from the nearby black shantytown known simply as The Location. It was the beginning of a deep relationship with the place and the local people.

'I love the place,' he said. 'The wave is like no other, the people are pure gold and it's maybe my favourite stop on the schedule.'

Mick won the event at Jeffreys Bay again in 2006 and 2014, and was runner-up in 2008 and 2011 (the event was not held in 2012 and 2013). He returned in 2015 as defending event champion, ranked fourth in the world. His progression to the final had already earned him the overall ratings lead and another win would have set Mick up for a record-equalling fourth world title. Then, a large fish intervened.

It has been described as the heaviest nine seconds in the history of sport. It has been compared to Tiger Woods being attacked by a hippopotamus at a water hazard or Roger Federer playing tennis among a pride of lions: an elite athlete, a three-time world champion no less, attacked by a wild animal in an international competition, broadcast live to living rooms around the globe.

'The last thing on my mind was a shark,' Mick explained at the press conference at Sydney Airport.

'I just had this instinct that something was behind me. All of a sudden I was getting pulled underwater and then the thing came up and I was on my board and it was right there – I saw the fin thrashing around and I was getting dragged under by my leg rope. It just sort of came up and went for the tail of my board. I don't know why it didn't bite but it just kept coming back. I was on top of it, trying to put my board between us.'

He realised he'd have to defend himself.

'I punched it a couple of times. I don't know if I punched it hard or if they were little baby punches but I just went into fight or flight. Then all of a sudden my leg rope broke. At that stage I was screaming. I was swimming in and I had this thought: "What if it comes to have another go at me?" I turned around and I was [floating] on my back and I was waiting for it. I had my fist cocked and I was ready to go.'

Nine seconds. It felt like a lifetime. The webcast audience saw little more than splashes obscured by waves, and feared the worst. They held their breath. The whole surfing world held its breath.

'I was thinking: "We're watching a three-time world champion die." That was the reality of the situation,' webcast commentator Ronnie Blakey told Triple M radio. 'At worst I thought if he isn't dead, maybe he's lost a limb.'

As abruptly as Mick disappeared, he suddenly re-appeared on the computer screen: a black dot circled by jetskis and rescue boats.

'He'll hop on the sled and reset,' co-commentator Joe Turpel intoned in a now infamous understatement.

Mick crouched on elbows and knees on the back of the jetski sled, his head in his hands, before holding up the chewed end of his leg rope in disbelief.

'I just felt so insignificant – the thing was so powerful and it just moved so fast,' he said. 'It sounds kind of stupid. The place where I went to heal was the ocean, the exact same place that nearly took my life.'

It was a miracle. Mick had survived the attack physically unscathed. In her Tweed Heads lounge room, between tears of joy and relief, Liz Osborne knew that her youngest son's guardian angel was watching over him, protecting him from harm.

'That's my Sean,' she said. 'Absolutely. His brother was keeping an eye out for him.'

10

SHARK ALLEY

SOUTH AFRICA HAS a reputation for sharks. It dates back to the summer of 1957, known as 'Black December', when there were nine attacks and six deaths in the space of 107 days along the 160-kilometre stretch of coast between Durban and Port Edward in KwaZulu-Natal province, known in tourist brochures as the Hibiscus Coast. The attacks had a devastating effect on the tourist-based economy of South Africa's second-biggest city and nearby coastal resort towns like Margate, Port Shepstone and Scottburgh, with holidaymakers fleeing the beach during peak summer season.

Fearing financial disaster, local authorities erected barriers to enclose swimming areas, while a navy frigate dropped depth charges, killing eight sharks but attracting many more to feed along a shoreline littered with dead fish. By 1962, the KwaZulu-Natal Sharks Board was formally established to 'safeguard bathers against shark attacks' and expand beach netting. By 1992,

37 beaches were protected by shark nets, covering a total of 45 kilometres of coastline.

There were 23 fatal shark attacks in KwaZulu-Natal province in the 20 years before the installation of nets. There have been two unprovoked attacks and no fatalities at protected beaches since.

The Wild Coast of the Transkei homelands, stretching south from the border of KwaZulu-Natal to East London, is a different story. The traditional home of the Xhosa people and the birthplace of Nelson Mandela, the Transkei was an independent republic from 1963 to 1994, and less than 1 per cent of the population is white. The sparsely populated Transkei coastline is remote and desolate – a jagged 250-kilometre shoreline of windswept beaches, towering coastal bluffs and sheer cliffs that plunge dramatically into the Indian Ocean and the fast-flowing Agulhas Current. While shark nets in KwaZulu-Natal province catch more than 1300 sharks each year, including almost 40 great whites, there are no shark nets across the border in the Transkei. Records of shark attacks in South Africa date back to the turn of the century, when a Boer prisoner of war was attacked and killed by a shark while bathing in the nude near Cape Town during the Boer War. However, there was very little record of shark attacks in the Transkei until the early 1980s.

On 29 June 1982, a great white shark attacked and killed well-known South African surf photographer Alex Macun at Breezy Point, an isolated right-hand point break in Ntlonyana Bay, at the heart of the Wild Coast and seven hours south of Durban. In one of South Africa's most infamous attacks, the shark dragged the 27-year-old from his surfboard and 'proceeded to savage his body', according to a detailed report by Marie Levine, founder of the Shark Research Institute.

> Two eyewitnesses watched the shark attacking and thrusting the victim's body towards the rocks where they were standing. At one stage the body was about three metres away from them, with the shark in between, but the water was so discoloured with blood that they were unable to assess the extent of Macun's injuries. The attack continued for more than an hour. Macun's body was never recovered.

The attack occurred just over a year after Durban surfer Simon Hammerton lost his leg at the same location at the same time of year, during the annual sardine run along the Transkei coast. Upon hearing of Macun's death, Hammerton expressed frustration that surfers continued to frequent 'that sharky point' during June and July, when marine life was most active.

'How many more people have to be attacked before they realise this?' he asked in *The Cape Times* newspaper.

However, Hammerton underestimated the lengths to which surfers will go, and the risks they will endure, all for a few waves.

Breezy Point was infamous in South African surfing circles, but the horror of Macun's attack had faded when, 15 years later, on 21 July 1997, Sydney surfer Mark Penches was attacked and killed there. After graduating from university with a degree in coastal management, the 25-year-old worked three jobs to save for his dream surf trip through Indonesia, Europe and Africa. He parted ways with his girlfriend in Europe and travelled on through Africa alone and near destitute – sleeping in a tent held together with duct tape, wrapped in stolen airline blankets, while living on two-minute noodles and hitching rides with fellow travellers in search of waves.

He had run out of money and was due to return home to Australia in a few weeks when his journey seemed to reach its high-water mark and he paddled out into an empty line-up of perfect surf at Ntlonyana Bay. Solid overhead swell was brushed by light offshore winds, and Penches caught some of the best waves of his life.

'Mark was surfing with wings,' American surfer Terry Gibson recalled later in *Surfing's Greatest Misadventures*, a collection of surf stories edited by Paul Diamond.

But as he began paddling back up the point after a long ride, Penches was attacked by a great white shark that launched him 5 metres into the air, seized his right leg and dragged him under. Gibson and Sydney surfer Clyde Crawford ran along the boulder-strewn shoreline to rescue him.

'I saw his head lolling about as if struggling for breath but there was no way to get to him – big surf broke right on the rocks,' Gibson said in *Surfing's Greatest Misadventures*.

Eventually, Gibson swam out through a channel in the rocks to retrieve Mark's lifeless body and, with Crawford's assistance, dragged it from the water. Mark's right leg was severed at the hip and still attached to his surfboard, his leg rope acting like a morbid umbilical cord. 'His forearms were in ribbons from fighting the shark. His wetsuit was ripped off at the waist. His genitals lay against a bloodless, cavernous hole where the leg had been torn from the hip.'

'The dynamic is familiar,' South African surf journalist Craig Jarvis explained in *Stab* magazine. 'An attack happens, the place becomes notorious, and thereafter its name is tainted by the spectre of the shark.'

Jarvis suggested that ever since Mark Penches' attack, 'most [surfers] are too scared' to surf Breezy Point. Consequently, the spectre moved 85 kilometres further north, to Second Beach at Port St Johns, a small tourist town of less than 7000 souls at the mouth of the Mzimvubu River. Second Beach saw two incidents in the 1950s and, after a lull of over 50 years, was the site of eight fatal shark attacks in the space of seven years, between 2007 and 2014.

The first fatality was local bodysurfer Siyabulela Masiza, who had been bitten on the calf in 2004 only to be attacked again in January 2007. The 24-year-old's body was never recovered and only one of his flippers was found, with the fine serrations on the flipper leading KwaZulu-Natal Sharks Board expert Geremy Cliff to tell *The Daily Dispatch* that the animal responsible could 'only have been a tiger shark'.

In 2009, two local lifeguards were attacked and killed by bull sharks. In late January, Sikhanyiso Bangilizwe's body was 'torn apart' in front of his friend and fellow lifeguard Tshintshekile Nduva.

'I heard his cries. I saw he was in trouble and the shark on him. I saw blood and I went out of the water to get help,' Nduva told Port Elizabeth newspaper *The Herald*.

The shark ripped Bangilizwe's body into three pieces, biting off his right arm, shoulder, part of his back and buttocks.

'His body was badly injured. We could see his insides. It was the scariest thing I have ever seen,' Nduva said. 'To see him die has made it difficult for me to sleep. I wish I could get pills so that I don't get troubled. I am not well, but I will continue to go into the water as a lifeguard.'

Nduva's job as a lifeguard was highly prized in the poor coastal community of Port St Johns and the 22-year-old was his family's main breadwinner. But clearly it was not without risk. Eleven months later, on 18 December, Nduva was pulled off his paddleboard by a bull shark and instantly killed in a vicious attack that 'turned [the water] blood red'.

Wild Coast Guards Managing Director Khaya Mijo wondered why the shark attacks were suddenly focused on Second Beach and asked *The Herald* journalist Mawande Jack, 'Why are only lifeguards the ones being attacked while nothing happens to ordinary people?'

Unfortunately, 'ordinary people' were not immune from the man-eating sharks, with three local surfers killed in the space of three years. In March 2009, 16-year-old surfer Luyolo Mangele had his legs mauled by a bull shark and died from loss of blood. In January 2011, 16-year-old surfer Zama Ndamase 'had a big chunk bitten off his right leg' by a tiger shark and died on the beach. In January 2012, 25-year-old surfer Ngidi Msungubana was repeatedly bitten on both arms by a bull shark and died before reaching the nearby Isilimela Hospital. It was the sixth fatal attack since 2007 and it prompted one Port St Johns lifeguard Nqobile Jojo to immediately resign.

'I can't do it any more. This is my life and my passion but I can't go back in the water,' Jojo told Johannesburg-based national newspaper *City Press*.

I was watching from the beach and I saw the water turning red around him. I blew my whistle and ran into the water to get the other people out. His board was floating and I grabbed it and tried to pull him onto it. We were in very shallow water – he was about waist deep when the shark took him. We got him out of the water. Then later I started shaking. I realised it could have been me. I'm flesh and bone like he was.

Unfortunately, there was little alternative employment in Port St Johns, which relies heavily on seasonal tourism.

'What choice do we have?' another lifeguard asked *City Press*. 'If we don't work at the beach, it's sit at home, steal crayfish or sell [marijuana]. There are no jobs here.'

And the town's 34 lifeguards were living up to their name – literally guarding people's lives from the increasing menace of killer sharks. Or not. Less than a year after Msungubana's death, on Christmas Day 2012, Liya Sibili from the nearby rural village of Ntsimbini was attacked and killed by a bull shark while swimming in waist-deep water. After a three-day search for the 22-year-old's body, only Liya's shorts were recovered.

Port St Johns' growing 'shark crisis' was having an enormous impact on the local black community, but was gaining little interest beyond – the victims were all young local Xhosa men. Then, in March 2014, retired Austrian politician Friedrich Burgstaller was attacked and killed while swimming with his wife Margit at Second Beach. The incident captured international media attention and Port St Johns was quickly dubbed 'the world's deadliest beach'. The 66-year-old was part of a tour group that had stopped in Port St Johns en route to Nelson Mandela's hometown, the rural village of Qunu. Standing in shallow water, Burgstaller was attacked by a 3-metre bull shark. He tried to hit the shark on the head with his right arm, but the shark bit it off. He was then dragged out to sea and spent the next 20 minutes fighting off the shark while trying to swim back to shore with one arm. Two off-duty lifeguards eventually swam out about 30 metres to retrieve Burgstaller's corpse. Six months later, in September 2014, South

Africa's Department of Environmental Affairs finally announced that it was investigating 'mitigation measures to address the spate of shark attacks in Port St Johns'.

'I have no doubt that one shark in a dozen years is enough to keep up the reputation of a beach a hundred miles long,' American philosopher Henry David Thoreau wrote in his 1865 book about Cape Cod.

One hundred and fifty years later, Mick Fanning's dramatic encounter with a great white shark at Jeffreys Bay gave Thoreau's theory teeth, once again putting South Africa's 'shark problem' in the spotlight, generating headlines around the world and spawning an avalanche of memes on social media, with popular US sports blog FanSided declaring Fanning as 'the world's biggest badass' for fighting off the shark. He was offered a spot on the twenty-third season of hit American reality TV show *Dancing with the Stars* and was spoofed in a Kentucky Fried Chicken commercial. South African–born actress Charlize Theron discussed the incident on popular American late-night talk show *Jimmy Kimmel Live*, amplifying the perception that South African beaches were literally swarming with sharks.

'When I was a kid I used to swim in those waters all the time,' she said.

> Regularly, I would say once a day, the lifeguard would blow his whistle and that just automatically meant that everybody had to leave the water. We would just swim out to the edge and stand on the sand, and we would watch the waves go up and watch the sharks swim by. And then another whistle would be blown and that was like: 'Okay, go on back.' And we did. We did. Isn't that insane? I don't want to single-handedly kill the tourism for Jeffreys Bay. It's beautiful but there were a lot of [shark] attacks.

The famous actress's comments drew a barrage of criticism in South Africa and seemed to bear little resemblance to reality, unless you subscribe to Vic Hislop conspiracy theories. There have only been four recorded shark attacks at Jeffreys Bay, including Fanning's most recent encounter. Geremy Cliff from the KwaZulu-Natal Sharks Board (KZNSB) said that shark attacks were 'rare' in a country with a population of 53 million people and a coastline of 2500 kilometres. An analysis of KZNSB statistics for the past 40 years indicates that there is an average of six shark attacks in South Africa each year – half as many as in Australia during the same period. In the past decade alone, there have been 40 unprovoked attacks in South Africa and 123 attacks in Australia.

'Since 1990, only twenty-six per cent of attacks [in South Africa] have resulted in serious injury and only fifteen per cent were fatal,' Cliff confirmed. 'This equates to an average of one serious shark-inflicted injury every year and one shark-inflicted fatality every 1.2 years.'

This compares with conservative estimates that lions kill at least 10 people in South Africa each year – most notably refugees from Mozambique crossing the border through Kruger National Park, but also tourists. Twenty-nine-year-old American tourist Katherine Chappell was mauled to death at Lion Park near Johannesburg just six weeks before Fanning was attacked at J-Bay. Comparatively, it passed like a blip on the mainstream media radar. Meanwhile, the black mamba snake is blamed for hundreds of deaths each year, hippos kill almost 3000 people across Africa annually, and the female Anopheles mosquito is responsible for the loss of almost 1 million lives through the spread of malaria. The shark barely rates in the top 10 deadliest animals in South Africa, coming in at number nine on the hit parade, below the elephant but above the rhinoceros.

Shark attacks at Jeffreys Bay, one of the country's most popular surfing destinations, are incredibly uncommon.

'I wouldn't regard Jeffreys Bay as being very sharky,' Cliff said.

J-Bay sits inside the curve of Cape St Francis on South Africa's Eastern Cape, 70 kilometres west of Port Elizabeth and almost 1000 kilometres south-west of Durban. The area's waves were first exposed in 1963, when Californian filmmaker Bruce Brown filmed Mike Hynson and Robert August riding the mythical 'perfect wave' at Cape St Francis, about 20 kilometres south-west of J-Bay, for his 1966 surf movie *The Endless Summer*. The sequence of Hynson and August scrambling across the sand dunes to discover flawlessly shaped waves that 'looked like they'd been made by some kind of machine' was the climax of Brown's groundbreaking movie, which sold out theatres across the US and cemented surfing's crossover into mainstream popular culture.

While the 1959 Hollywood adaption of Frederick Kohner's teen novel *Gidget* had been followed by a wave of popular 'surfsploitation films' like *Beach Party* (1963), *Ride the Wild Surf* (1964) and *Beach Blanket Bingo* (1965), *The Endless Summer* was radically different in that it captured something of the true essence of surfing and the search for the perfect wave. Brown suggested the odds of actually finding a perfect wave like Cape St Francis were '10 million to one', compared to the odds *National Geographic* cites for being attacked by a shark: 3.7 million to one.

'That's just the lemon next to the pie,' as Bear, the weather-beaten old salt, growled cryptically in John Milius's cult coming-of-age surf film *Big Wednesday*.

And so it was. An article in *Surfer* magazine in 1968 revealed that Cape St Francis was fickle but introduced the surfing world to a much better alternative in nearby Jeffreys Bay: a small Afrikaner fishing village that boasted a long, fast, right-hand point break far superior to Cape St Francis in every way.

'Back then there were no homes on the beachfront, there was absolutely nothing, it was just sand dunes and the bush,' South Africa's 1977 world surfing champion Shaun Tomson recalled on the World Surf League website.

> I remember it so clearly. My first surf at J-Bay was absolutely magic. I was about twelve years old. The surf was perfect, four to five feet, and no-one out. I've been in love with Jeffreys Bay ever since.

J-Bay is the sort of place that induces infatuation. A natural wonder of the world, it is renowned for its incredible waves and active marine life, where large pods of hundreds of dolphins chase swells down the aloe-lined point, migrating southern right whales drift through the wide bay, and great whites and bull sharks are 'an ever-present threat', according to Matt Warshaw's *Encyclopedia of Surfing*. Although J-Bay is one of the world's premier waves and has attracted a steady stream of gypsy surfers like Mark Penches since the early 1970s, the first recorded shark attack wasn't until July 1989, when local surfer Roniel 'Koffie' Jacobs was bumped from his surfboard by a great white. Thirteen days later, Johannesburg surfer Edward Razzano was bitten on the upper thigh and bum. Razzano described it as a 'gentle, investigatory bite', albeit one that required more than 100 stitches.

'I wasn't sure it was a shark,' Razzano told Jeffreys Bay community newspaper *Our Times*. 'I thought it might have been a dolphin gone mad.'

Then, in October 2013, long-distance swimmer Burgert van der Westhuizen was bitten in half in a horrific attack near the end section of the famous surf break. The 74-year-old was attacked in shallow water close to the rocks, two-thirds of the way through his daily morning swim. Local surfer Terry Olivier was paddling in his surf ski when he noticed people waving and screaming on the shore. Built like a silverback gorilla, with long, ropey arms, a prominent potbelly and a curving handlebar moustache, Terry isn't scared of much on God's green earth. So he paddled out to where a flock of seabirds was diving into the water.

'There was this body, just shoulders and head, bobbing up,' Terry told Afrikaans-language newspaper *Die Burger*.

> The shark was circling, eating, circling, eating. I thought I'd try and grab the body and put it on the ski but as I got closer the shark came out of the water and just took the whole body. Then I saw the size of it. My ski is five metres and it was longer than my ski. It circled me a bit and I thought it didn't look good. The chap was dead. He had no arms. His legs were gone. So I turned around and sprinted in … Then the rescue jetski came and chased the shark away.

'People say that South Africa is dangerous, but I always feel safe there,' Mick Fanning said in *Surf for Your Life* in 2009.

If anything, back then Mick was more afraid of the high rate of violent crime than sharks – the rates of assault, murder, rape and carjacking in South Africa are ranked among the highest in the world by the United Nations. 'This one time I was in Durban and, you know, there's a lot of poverty there in the city. I remember walking up after a surf in the morning and this kid was just shaking his mate because his mate had overdosed on glue.'

Glue sniffing is endemic among South African street kids and in poor black communities. Glue is inexpensive, readily available and provides a short jolt of joy in an otherwise bleak existence. It also suppresses feelings of hunger and cold, but few users, many of whom are children as young as seven or eight, understand the risks.

'I think [seeing] that was the thing that affected me the most because that could have been one of my friends. That could have been anyone.'

He may be a famous surf star, but Mick has been exposed to a far darker, more complex seam of South African life than most tourists ever get to glimpse. In 2005, he befriended Primrose Manyangaza, the black maid who was working as a cleaner at the J-Bay house where he and his mum, Liz, were staying.

'She was pregnant at the time and we just got talking to her about how much money she gets paid and stuff like that,' Mick said. 'She told us that she didn't even make enough money to be able to go and buy nappies for the baby that was coming.'

So Liz went out and bought a box of nappies and clothes for the baby, which was born three months later. Like almost 30 per cent of all pregnant women in South Africa, Primrose had HIV/ AIDS. Six months later the baby died and Primrose's health began deteriorating.

'That was pretty heartbreaking, so we started sending money for medication.'

Primrose contracted an eye disease and started going blind. Mick paid for an operation to save her sight. He helped Primrose set up a hair salon with her sister Timbaland, which provided work and an income for other women in The Location. He helped pay for her to study counselling in Port Elizabeth, and Primrose now helps with blood testing and counselling for other people living with HIV/AIDS.

'It is really cool, just to see her wanting to give back to the community,' Mick said.

Primrose explained in *Surf for Your Life*:

This is God's work. Sometimes when you believe in Him, good things happen. I just fell in love with [Mick and Liz] and they fell in love with me. They were trying to look after me. When I was sick, they were there. I am fine. Before I was not, but now I am.

Mick didn't want to promote the support he provided for Primrose and her local community at The Location, where he is treated as a hero and church services are held in his honour, but he desperately wanted to continue surfing at Jeffreys Bay despite the attack.

'I want to go back to J-Bay and I want to leave on a positive note, not a negative one,' he said. 'It is a place where I have so many amazing memories. I just feel it's a place where I want to right the wrong. It's something that I've got to do for myself. It's going to be hard but you have got to face these things front on.'

On Monday 27 June 2016, Mick Fanning returned to Jeffreys Bay.

'The first thing was just getting out there again,' Mick said. 'A little bit of anxiety sort of came up and a few different emotions. But once I got the wetsuit on and got the board ready and paddled out, it was pretty much fine. Once you catch that first wave, you realise that it was just a one-off incident, hopefully, then you just get on with it and go surfing again.'

Following a turbulent 2015, Mick took a break from competitive surfing at the beginning of 2016. After surviving the shark attack in South Africa and subsequent media frenzy, Mick needed some time 'to find me again'. Following months of media speculation, he ended his eight-year marriage to Karissa Dalton. He travelled to Hawaii for the season-ending Pipe Masters locked in a nail-biting world title race with Brazilian surfers Filipe Toledo, Adriano de Souza and Gabriel Medina.

While preparing for competition at the notorious Banzai Pipeline, Mick was involved in the dramatic rescue of 22-year-old Floridian surfer Evan Geiselman, who was dragged unconscious from the water after a horrific wipeout and rushed to hospital in a critical condition. Then, just before he paddled out for his third-round heat against Pipeline heavyweights 11-time world champion Kelly Slater and four-time Volcom Pipe Pro winner John John Florence, Mick was told that his eldest brother, 43-year-old Peter, had died of a heart attack while staying in Fanning's Gold Coast home. Remarkably, Mick won the heat but lost to Medina in the semifinals, while de Souza won the event and the world title.

'I think Mick deserved it more than me,' de Souza said during his victory speech. 'He's such a strong man – the strongest man I have met in my whole life.'

After 15 years on surfing's elite World Championship Tour, 21 event wins and three world titles, Mick announced that 2016 would be a 'personal year'; that he would only compete in a select handful of events, with a particular focus on the J-Bay Open. While some surfers had questioned the future of the event after Fanning's high-profile shark incident, Mick lobbied hard for it to retain its place on surfing's Championship Tour.

'It was definitely emotional, even just paddling out,' he admitted. 'But how could we not have come back to J-Bay?'

Mick arrived in Jeffreys Bay a week before the event began to rekindle his 'special' relationship with the famous surf break, only to badly sprain his ankle on his second day in South Africa, casting doubts on whether he would be able to compete at all. Those doubts were erased with an emphatic first-round win. Fanning followed up with the highest heat total of round three, before blitzing Filipe Toledo in the quarterfinals to set up an emotionally charged rematch with Julian Wilson in the semis. If circumstances were not already surreal enough, Julian caught the first wave of the semifinal, leaving Mick alone on the line-up, floating motionlessly on the horizon for almost five minutes. Lightning did not strike twice. Mick caught a wave and flew down the point with trademark frenetic energy, slashing, bashing and clearly out-pointing his younger rival.

'Having a semi with Julian, that was really special,' he said later, during a World Surf League post-event interview. 'He's a great guy. He's just one of those guys who always has your back. It's just really special to have friends like that.'

Mick Fanning completed his fairytale return to Jeffreys Bay by defeating Hawaiian tyro John John Florence in the final of the J-Bay Open. When the siren sounded, Mick saluted the crowd, put his head in his hands and drifted beyond the breaking waves like a corpse, drained of life. His mum, Liz, and much-loved local friend Primrose stood side-by-side in the stands, tears streaming down their cheeks. It was 15 July 2016 – four days shy of the one-year anniversary of when Mick was almost eaten alive by a great white shark at this very spot in the ocean, on the edge of the take-off zone at Jeffreys Bay.

'I'm just so stoked to be able to come back, to right the wrong,' he said. 'That was my whole plan – to right the wrong that happened last year. We did that now, so we can move on.'

But the great white sharks at Jeffreys Bay didn't move on. When Fanning returned for the 2017 J-Bay Open, there were more shark sightings, courtesy of the aerial drones and patrol boats employed by the World Surf League (WSL) to monitor the surf break during the event. Competition was cancelled during round four when a two-metre mako shark breached the water 100 metres from Julian Wilson. 'The first thing I think about is family, my wife, people that are close to me,' Julian told the WSL webcast. 'I want to just think about them, make sure they're OK and know that I'm fine. For me, it's just going out there and doing what I love.'

Then, during Mick's quarter-final with Gabriel Medina, the drone spotted a 3-metre great white swimming towards the surfers. Fanning and Medina were plucked from the water by jet-skis while the shark swam languidly up the point. 'I didn't actually see anything,' Mick admitted to *Surfer* magazine. 'I was out the back and heard the horns and that's when I knew they'd spotted something. They tracked it from way down the point so they had time to get us all out of the water no worries. But it was pretty wild to see it cruise through the whole line-up like that.'

Later, when Mick watched the aerial footage of the shark swimming casually across the bay, seemingly uninterested in the patrol boats, jet-skis and shoreline grandstands, he wondered how often great white sharks lurked dangerously below the surface at Jeffreys, unseen. 'At least they saw this one,' he said. 'I'm glad they got us out of the water. Those things are just submarines, however long they are, the roundness of them as well … they are big, big beasts.'

11

NOT TODAY DAVE

MICK FANNING STILL has nightmares.

'I guess when something like this happens, you are in your own mind and your mind can play tricks on you,' he said. 'Your mind can turn shadows into demons. I have nightmares. I get flashbacks and stuff like that. I guess the worst thing for me was seeing different angles of footage. I was explaining what happened when that wave came, what people didn't see, and at one point I thought: "Am I making this shit up?" It wasn't until I found some photos that backed up my story, which was awesome, like: "I'm not crazy." Then, when I did the story for *60 Minutes*, the cameraman came up from underneath me. In that footage I could see the silhouette of my board and me just sitting there, which really freaked me out because I suddenly had the vision of what the shark would've seen. It was a couple of weeks after [the attack] and I thought I was actually pretty good by then. Then I freaked out again. You have different self-doubts, like: "Why did I get away with that?" You look at it in so many different ways that you can get lost in it. Are you going to sit in that moment or are you going to take a step forward and keep moving on with life? I was always going to move on with life.'

Fifty-two-year-old Coopernook surfer Dave Pearson has not only moved on with life; his own brutal shark attack at Crowdy Bay on the mid-north coast of New South Wales in 2011 has been the driving force for a new life. The attack inspired Dave to establish Bite Club, a support group that helps other shark attack survivors, their rescuers, families and friends. Bite Club has almost 300 members, including more than 50 who have been bitten by a shark. It is an exclusive club, but not one with a long waiting list. Dave does not want new members, yet he actively seeks them out. As soon as he hears of a shark attack, he contacts the local hospital and asks to speak to the victim. He is also active on social media, and Bite Club has built a network of Facebook friends right around Australia.

'We want to use our own experiences to help families that have been affected by shark attacks and assist survivors through peer support,' he explained. 'We are very focused on mental health. When I meet people in hospital I hardly ever ask about the attack or the injuries. The first thing I ask them is: "Have you seen a counsellor?" We have got a great healthcare system in Australia but when you're in hospital they focus on the physical injuries. They turf you out and give you a handful of drugs for the pain. Eventually I went and saw a psychologist. That helped me a lot, but it would've been nice to know that up front, when I was in hospital.'

Dave Pearson is one of the friendliest guys you'll ever meet. There is something of the Walt Disney cartoon character Goofy about him, but in the best possible way, with his wide, toothy grin and infectious optimism.

'I have lived my life by the "glass half full" philosophy,' Dave said. 'I know people a whole lot worse off than me, so I think to myself: "Suck it up and have a go." Everybody has their own challenges, but when I'm having a bad day, I count all the good things in my life.'

One is living beside the beach in Australia, in the tiny village of Coopernook, which sits on a bend of the northern arm of the Manning River, near its mouth at Harrington Inlet.

Dave was born in Hartlepool, an ancient port on the edge of the North Sea in north-east England, where his father Chris was a telephone engineer. Hartlepool was a hub for shipbuilding and steel works – German bombers raided the town 43 times during World War II due to its strategic significance – but when those industries went into decline in the early 1970s, unemployment skyrocketed and 'it became a depressing place with decaying buildings and old redundant works'. 'Then there was one particularly bad winter when there was a lot of snow and I had to dig the driveway out every morning just to get the car out,' Chris recalled in his distinctive Durham accent. He promptly packed up his young family and moved to Sydney for a 'better life', settling in Seven Hills in Sydney's west when Dave was six years old.

'We always went down to the ocean on weekends,' Chris said. 'We went to Manly or the national park, but always to the beach. Dave and his brother and sister loved the ocean. I can remember them learning to surf at Wattamolla Beach. It is this little beach in a tiny cove with small waves, and that's where they first started getting up on their surfboards.'

Like most Australian kids in the 1970s, Dave started surfing on a polystyrene foam surfboard purchased for $2 with a bucket of Kentucky Fried Chicken. He quickly developed an obsessive relationship with surfing and a bottomless passion for the Pacific Ocean.

'Every weekend we were down at the beach, at least getting a couple of surfs in, and the ocean became the place where I took my problems,' he explained. 'We've had some pretty bad things happen in our family over the years. Both of my dad's brothers were involved in motor vehicle accidents, my dad was crushed by a forklift, my brother had his knee ripped off by a motorbike, my sister had breast cancer, while my partner and I lost a baby when we were younger. The ocean was always the place I went when I wasn't having a good day. I got away from all the problems in my life by going surfing. I've never done anything but love the ocean. And then it nearly killed me.'

On 23 March 2011, Dave raced straight from work (where he is an engineer in the mining industry) to his local surf break at Crowdy Head, 20 kilometres from Coopernook, for a late afternoon splash. He had a new surfboard – a futuristic Firewire design with high-density foam, aerospace epoxy construction and 12-millimetre-thick parabolic balsawood rails (most surfboards are constructed of polyurethane foam with a wooden stringer down the middle of the board, rather than around the outer edge). There were three other surfers in the water, including 27-year-old Aaron 'Noddy' Wallis, whom Dave has known 'since he was a little snotty kid'. Dave entered the water at around quarter to six and caught a good wave almost immediately. 'It was a really good wave. As I was paddling back out I was thinking: "This board feels pretty good" … it was fast and loose. I was paddling back out, looking at where Noddy was sitting, and [the shark] just charged me. I didn't see it coming at all. It charged up from the bottom and it must've been flying – it felt like being hit by a train.

The board hit me in the head and the impact was just unbeliev-able. The best way to describe it would be if you were driving through an intersection, looking to your left, and someone comes straight through and T-bones you from the right-hand side at fifty kilometres an hour. That's sort of what it was like. All I saw was a grey flash.'

This was when Dave's new surfboard saved his life. The 3-metre bull shark's nose bashed into Dave's ribs and it latched onto his right arm, dragging him underwater, but its bottom teeth got stuck in the surfboard's unique balsawood rails.

'I was so lucky because its teeth were stuck in the bottom of the surfboard and it couldn't bite down,' Dave said. 'It just caught my forearm in its mouth. My thumb went into its mouth but my fingers were on the outside. If my arm had gone down its throat it would've been a whole different story.'

Noddy was 15 metres away from Dave and heard the colli-sion, which 'sounded like fibreglass snapping'. 'He said that he looked over and thought: "Shit, wasn't Dave there a second ago?" Then my surfboard popped up. A few seconds later I swam to the surface and I got back on my board. I don't remember a lot of that or what happened afterwards. I remember looking at my arm, at the flesh ripped open and the white bone, and thinking: "Shit, that don't look good." Then I was watching the blood squirt out of my veins and thinking: 'Gee, the water is going red.' It was then that it dawned on me that it was a shark. The water was quite clear and I could actually see [the shark] underneath me, swimming around.'

'It all happened so quickly, just so fast,' Noddy told the local *Manning River Times*. 'I said: "That was a shark wasn't it?" Then I started yelling, alerting everyone else in the water and asking for someone to come and help. Then I started paddling over to

Dave but he told me not to come over because the shark was still there.'

Dave remembered: 'Noddy was screaming at me. I was sitting there like an idiot, stunned and half conscious. I said to him: "It's still here so get the fuck out, I'll be alright." I tried to stop the bleeding the best I could and turned to paddle. A decent set came through and broke right on top of me and I got driven down into the impact zone. As I came back to the surface I was trying to put the flap on my arm back together and then the next wave hit me. All I was thinking was: "My skin is going to fall off and I'm going to be buggered." Another wave hit me and I thought: "Shit, I'm drowning." I realised then that I'd lost all my strength and that I was going to die. I was actually sort of okay with it. Then I said to myself: "Not today Dave. I've got kids. I've got a partner. Nup. Not today." I pushed myself back up. I got on my board just as another set of waves was coming and I heard Noddy say: "Come on Dave, we're here and we're going to get you out."'

'I didn't want to be there,' Noddy confessed to *The Daily Telegraph*. 'I didn't want to die. The whole time I was thinking: "Shit, this thing is still here." First I told him to try and paddle in himself but he just couldn't. Then I thought he could hold on to my leg and I'd drag him with me, but he was too weak to do that as well. So I started pushing him and then paddling after him, before a big set came in that would take him through the trough. He could hardly hold on … but once we got past that trough there were people waiting for us.'

'They reckon it took about 15 minutes from the time I was attacked until I was back on the beach,' Dave said. 'I'd lost quite a bit of blood. They dragged me up the beach and threw me on a picnic table. I spent an hour on that picnic table with my mates keeping me alive until the ambulance got there. It was another hour, hour and a half, by the time they stabilised me and got me off the picnic table and into the chopper.'

Noddy used his leg rope as a temporary tourniquet around Dave's arm. Adam Eady, the caretaker of the Crowdy Head Surf Life Saving Club, arrived with oxygen and first aid. Eventually the rescue helicopter flew Dave to Newcastle's John Hunter Hospital, where he underwent five hours of emergency surgery.

'A lot of people die from losing that much blood,' intensive care paramedic Alan Playford told the *Manning River Times* later.

Meanwhile, news of Dave's attack spread across social media.

'I got hammered on the internet, on social media and in newspaper comments, and that really took me by surprise,' Dave said.

He was criticised for surfing at dusk, for surfing during mullet season, for surfing three weeks after a nearby beach had been closed because of shark sightings and for simply 'having the audacity to go into the ocean and get attacked'.

'It's the shark's ocean. It's his own fault he got attacked. He shouldn't have been there,' a typical comment read.

Dave initially responded to each negative comment, defending his actions, but has since realised that the level of hostility directed towards survivors is just another consequence of shark attacks. 'It gets personal and it gets really aggressive. It's just one more thing that you have to deal with. When you're in hospital it is a big deal. For me, there was a media circus and it was: "Look at me, I'm special." But I was no more special than anyone else in that hospital. I was just a patient. Then you go home and you're left sitting on your lounge when everyone else has had to go back to work and get on with their own life. We [shark attack survivors] are fish and chip wrappers in a few days and forgotten about after that. But the support I received from my family and my partner Debbie was brilliant. It allowed me to keep going and help others.'

It began before Dave had even left John Hunter Hospital. Seven days before Dave's attack, 24-year-old wakeboarder Lisa Mondy had been attacked by a great white shark at Jimmys Beach on the sheltered northern shore of Port Stephens. 'I was actually down near Port Stephens when she was attacked and saw the chopper flying over to the hospital afterwards. I remember hearing it on the radio and feeling really bad that this poor young girl had been attacked and nearly died. Then the next week I'm in the same hospital as her. The day I was going home I went and chatted with her. They were changing the dressings on her arms and we compared scars. It intrigued me how differently we were dealing with it. For me, as an old guy, it was another event in my life. For Lisa, as a young girl, it was the worst thing that had ever happened to her. I could put it into perspective, having lost a child and all the other things that have happened, but it really messed Lisa up. And fair enough.'

When a bull shark attacked 44-year-old tattoo artist Glen Folkard while surfing at Redhead Beach south of Newcastle on 18 January 2012, Dave sought him out in hospital. 'I heard his interview on the radio and he did not sound well at all, so I thought: "I've got to go and meet this guy." I went and spent a few hours in hospital with him and shared a few things I'd been through and some of the signs to watch out for.'

From there, it snowballed. Dave got in contact with David Pickering, who was attacked by a tiger shark while snorkelling at Ningaloo Reef in Western Australia the day after Glen Folkard's attack. Pickering put Dave in contact with Elyse Frankcom, who was bitten by a great white shark while scuba diving at Garden

Island off the coast of Rockingham in Western Australia on 30 October 2010. Then he made contact with 20-year-old Gold Coast surfer Billy O'Leary, who was bitten on the calf after landing on a bull shark while surfing at Nobby Beach on 20 March 2012.

'We suddenly had all these people who had been attacked and we were all learning from each other and it was really good.'

But contacting shark attack survivors in hospital didn't always go smoothly. When Dave rang Dale Carr after a great white shark attacked the Port Macquarie bodyboarder at Lighthouse Beach on 22 August 2015, Carr thought Dave was a 'lunatic'.

'I was in my hospital bed and he rang up and said: "It's Dave Pearson here from Bite Club",' Dale told ABC Mid North Coast radio. 'I thought it was a dead set joke. I actually hung up on him the first time he called and told my friend that some weirdo had just phoned me up and said he was from Bite Club!'

Carr has since become one of Bite Club's most active members. 'The first words that Dave said to me really resonated. He said: "You'll be right buddy, there are plenty of people around you that can support you." The first rule of Bite Club is to talk about Bite Club. An attack can leave you with post-traumatic stress for years afterwards and as a group it's important that we can talk about our issues when they arise.'

It wasn't long after his attack that Dave began dreaming of getting back into the ocean. But he was having some other 'funny dreams' as well. 'I only remember little bits of the attack, which I'm sort of grateful for, but other bits came back through dreams. Because your mind is so focused on survival in that moment, it blocks things out that are too heavy to deal with, so it was hard for me to tell what was real. One Sunday, my partner, Debbie, was home and I dozed off on the lounge. The dog started barking and I woke up screaming. It scared me. It scared me that I was doing that and Debbie said: "I've got to get you some help." I went to a psychologist and I had lots of questions.'

Ten weeks after the attack, Dave paddled back out into the line-up at Crowdy Bay on Debbie's soft foam surfboard. He still couldn't put any weight on his arm, so he couldn't actually surf, but he was strong enough to paddle and he needed some answers.

'I managed to paddle out to the same location where I was attacked. I sat there and had a conversation with the ocean. I said: "I'm not going to hold any grudges here, let's leave this today and let's move on." It was for me. It was weird. But it was to allow me to keep going.'

Dave has kept going. He still surfs at every opportunity, often with a small group of fellow Bite Club members like Dale Carr and Bruce Lucas from nearby Cundletown, but the memory of the attack never fully disappears. 'It is with me every time I paddle out. It is with me every time there is a shark attack – I go back there and I remember what happened to me that day and I remember what my family went through. My heart just stops for a second.'

The sharks don't disappear either. In the past six years, Dave has had a number of close encounters, including being chased from the water by an aggressive bull shark while surfing with his son. 'Mentally, that was a nasty experience for me. I sat on the beach and thought: "I can't do this anymore." That was a defining moment when I decided that it wasn't going to get to me and I wasn't going to give up.'

Chris Pearson admires his son's commitment to surfing despite the inherent dangers. 'He's always loved the ocean,' Chris said.

'First thing in the morning, he's out there. And it's marvellous to watch – he's really enjoying himself. [The shark attack] was a terrible shock. It's one of those things that always happens to someone else. It's the same as a car accident. If you drive a car, you can have an accident. If you sit home and do nothing, nothing will happen to you. He is a caring lad, so I understand what he's doing [with Bite Club], but I'm a little bit surprised how far it has gone.'

Bite Club has captured the country's imagination. It has featured on Channel 7's *Sunday Night* program (where members swam with sharks at Manly Aquarium) and *Four Corners* on the ABC. It has established a national committee and was recently registered as a charitable organisation with the Australian Charities and Not-for-profits Commission.

'We're getting our act together,' Dave said. 'One of our aims is to raise funds for survivors and their families. We're also working with mental health professionals to identify what is required. We've been to see government because we want to help them develop policy. Our vision is to get our survivors back to a normal life. It will never be the same as it was, but you've got to make it normal again and accept your new normal. It's also about looking after everybody that's involved in the attack. The witnesses and the rescuers actually see a lot more than what the survivors do. I was just trying to get out of the water to save my life, but Noddy had to consciously make a decision about how to act, what to do, if he was going to intervene or not. To make that decision, to step in and risk his life to help me, is a big call.'

The magnitude of Noddy's action hit home when Mick Fanning was attacked at Jeffreys Bay in South Africa, with fellow competitor Julian Wilson hailed as a hero for paddling to Fanning's assistance. 'I woke up and my phone had a thousand

A great white shark breaches in an attack.
Photo courtesy Sergey Uryadnikov/Alamy Stock Photo

The endangered oceanic whitetip shark is considered to be one of the most dangerous and unpredictable shark species.
Photo courtesy Nature Picture Library/Alamy Stock Photo

Despite its terrifying teeth, the sand tiger shark (grey nurse shark) is not considered particularly aggressive or dangerous.
Photo courtesy Michael Patrick O'Neill/Alamy Stock Photo

Bullsharks are thought to be the most dangerous shark on earth, based on the number of humans they have attacked.
Photo courtesy Michael Patrick O'Neill/Alamy Stock Photo

A great white marks the entrance of Vic Hislop's Shark Show.
Photo courtesy John Warburton-Lee Photography/Alamy Stock Photo

Bethany Hamilton at the Surfing Womens Festival, Phillip Island, Victoria, Australia
Photo courtesy Zuma Press, Inc/Alamy Stock Photo

Dave Pearson (at left), who set up Bite Club, with fellow shark attack survivor Dale Carr
Photo courtesy James Brickwood/Fairfax Syndication

Brooke Mason was surfing with Tadashi Nakahara at Shelly Beach, Ballina, in far northern New South Wales, when he was attacked by a shark, which bit off both of his legs.
Photo courtesy Brooke Mason

Inset: Darren Rogers rescued Tadashi Nakahara's body from the surf and attempted to provide first aid, but Tadashi died on the sand.
Photo courtesy Darren Rogers

Surf rescue boats search for the shark, believed to be a great white, which attacked Tadashi Nakahara at Shelly Beach.
Photo courtesy James Brickwood/Fairfax Syndication

There have been an unprecedented number of shark attacks off the shores of the idyllic island of Réunion. Many have lost loved ones in 'the shark crisis'.
Hemis/Alamy Stock Photo

A tiger shark is caught during a shark cull at Réunion Island.
Photo courtesy James Brickwood/Fairfax Syndication

Shark lover, conservationist and underwater filmmaker Madison Stewart swims with sharks.
Top: Photo courtesy Madison Stewart/Juan Medina
Bottom: Photo courtesy Madison Stewart/Pia Oyarzun

Shark attack survivor and advocate Mike Coots surfs with a prosthetic leg.
A professional photographer, he captures breathtaking shots of his surfing adventures with a GoPro camera.
Top and bottom photos courtesy Mike Coots

messages: "Did you see the Mick Fanning thing last night?" I hadn't but Noddy rang me and said: "Dave, it's only just sunk in what we did that afternoon." I'd been making a big deal out of it for four years and he was always brushing me aside, saying it was nothing. Now he knew just what a big thing it was.'

12

IT BEGAN IN BALLINA

WE ARE BACK in Ballina. The year is 1989 and the Fanning family has arrived in town, having driven an old red Datsun SS sedan from the western suburbs of Sydney to settle in a curve of Cedar Crescent, a stone's throw from Lighthouse Beach and the perfect curling waves of North Wall. This is the promised land that Liz Osborne has dreamed of for her three surf-mad sons, where the Pacific Ocean sparkles beyond the thickets of bitou bush, banksia and drooping casuarina. Liz has quit her job as a nurse to take up a position in the Mental Health Unit of the Lismore Base Hospital, 30 kilometres inland from Ballina. Her father was born in Ballina in Ireland, at the mouth of the River Moy. Consequently, the northern New South Wales town with the same name has always held a special place in her heart. She sits on the edge of the dunes, carpeted with dense swards of marram grass and hairy spinifex, with the sounds of her boys playing happily in the shore break floating on the breeze. This feels like the perfect place to start again.

'That was the happiest time of my life,' Liz told Tim Baker in *Surf for Your Life*. 'That was the happiest time of all our lives, living in Ballina.'

Mick, Sean and Ed Fanning had discovered surfing while living briefly with their estranged father John in Coffs Harbour. Liz encouraged the pursuit when they moved back to live with her in Bradbury, near Campbelltown in Sydney's west, driving them to the beach on weekends. The boys' older siblings Rachel and Peter had left the family nest and moved on to tertiary study. Liz took a leap of faith and moved on too, heading north for the sun, sand and surf. Mick was eight years old. He and Sean learned to surf on the big east swells that pushed up the Richmond River and rolled gently onto the shallow sandbank under the Missingham Bridge – the 'surfing kindergarten' for generations of local surfers.

'It was pretty eerie surfing under there as cars whizzed by overhead,' Mick recalled in *Surf for Your Life*. 'And we got chased in by sharks a few times.'

Mick and Sean soon progressed to the bigger waves of North Wall and the Fanning house became ground zero for a gang of skinny, knock-kneed, pre-teen surf groms, sunburnt, with peeling noses and hair tangled like seaweed. 'Everyone used our house as base camp. We had a huge garage and everyone left their surfboards there. We surfed North Wall all the time but we'd surf all along that stretch of coast – North Wall, South Wall, Speeds, Flat Rock. Wherever we could get to, that's where we would go.'

They joined the Le-Ba Boardriders Club and began surfing in local competitions. When Mick was 12, Liz got a job at the Gold Coast Hospital and the family moved north again, to Tweed

Heads and Coolangatta, to Palm Beach Currumbin High School, to Kirra Surfriders Club, Duranbah and Snapper Rocks. The rest is history. But Mick never forgot his surfing roots and, over the next few decades, dozens of surf films featured an obligatory few shots of Fanning at Ballina, arcing backside snaps at South Wall or weaving through overhead tubes at nearby Lennox Head. It became his rural idyll – an escape from the hustle and bustle of the Gold Coast and its increasingly overcrowded waves.

'To tell you the truth, I was actually planning on going down the day that Matty Lee got hit [on 2 July 2015]. When that happened, I got a text from a friend that someone got hit and I thought: "Oh no, I hope it's not one of the boys." That was the last time that I really thought about going down there. At that stage I didn't really know exactly who had been hit. The next day I was thinking I might go down and surf Lennox because there were good waves down there. But then it was like: "Nah, not worth the risk." And I haven't been back since.'

Mick's celebrated shark encounter at Jeffreys Bay in South Africa occurred just 17 days after Ballina bodyboarder Matt Lee was mauled by a 4-metre great white shark at North Wall. The 32-year-old underwent emergency surgery to save his legs and was placed in an induced coma, spending more than two months in Gold Coast Hospital – the very same hospital where Mick's mum, Liz, was a nurse all those years ago. While Matt was laid up in hospital, undergoing further surgery to his badly damaged left leg, Mick made an appearance on *60 Minutes*, recounting his skirmish at J-Bay. He then donated his $75,000 appearance fee to the Matt Lee Trust. 'There has been so many attacks [in Ballina], you are freaked out. People start saying: "I'm not going to go surfing there." It's scary, for sure. My mates are going out surfing with jetskis. The jetski is searching [for sharks] out the back while the others surf, and then they swap over. Speaking to the boys down there, they're definitely freaked out. When it keeps happening and you get these sightings all the time, you've got to be questioning something.'

Mick began questioning if Liz would have ever allowed him and his brothers to surf in Ballina amid so much shark activity. 'Probably not,' he concluded. 'She's really worried now [after the attack at Jeffreys Bay]. But out of all the days that I've gone surfing, to have one incident in thirty-five years, given the amount of hours I've spent in the water, is actually pretty good odds.'

But the odds of being attacked by a shark in Ballina were high. A remarkable 9 per cent of the world's total shark attacks in 2015 happened in the Ballina Shire, which boasts a population of just over 41,000 people. The local newspaper, *The Northern Star*, suggested that you were 153,846.154 times more likely to be attacked by a shark if you lived in Ballina than anywhere else on the planet. According to local marine ecologist Dr Daniel Bucher, those odds were dialled up a notch if you were in the water at dawn or dusk, during a full moon, or near the mouth of a river, particularly after rain or when the water was murky.

'It is that sort of equation where the risk is a lot higher than at other times,' Dr Bucher explained. 'We tend to think of shark attacks as a summer phenomenon and the issue we have when the water is warmer is the bull sharks, not the great whites. They are the problem. They are conditioned to feed at dawn and dusk, and they patrol that area where the deep water meets the shallow sandbanks. That's exactly where the surfers are sitting to wait for the next wave, so they are the ones who are most at risk.'

Enter 20-year-old Ballina surfer Sam Morgan, who was attacked by a 3-metre bull shark an hour before sunset while surfing at North Wall on 10 November 2015. Sam was the fourteenth person to be attacked by a shark on the north coast of New South Wales in 2015 and the fifth to be attacked along the 3.5-kilometre stretch of beach between North Wall and Black Head, the low rocky headland at the northern end of Shelly Beach. Sam was bitten on the left thigh and managed to make his own way to shore before being airlifted to Gold Coast Hospital, where he underwent emergency surgery and was placed in an induced coma.

'North Wall wasn't surfed at all for four months after Matt Lee's attack, until November, and then Sam was attacked,' Ballina mayor David Wright said. 'Sam's dad works in the shire's finance department, so to have someone that you know very well attacked, it was frightening.'

Heavy rain in the days before the attack had flushed muddy water and nutrient-rich run-off from the farming properties upriver out of the Richmond River mouth, sparking heightened marine activity and creating the low visibility that increases the risk of bull shark attacks.

'I've advocated so many times to not surf North Wall when we've had rain,' Le-Ba Boardriders Club president Don Munro said. 'It was a terrible situation but [Sam] works all day like all of us. You surf early and you surf late. It is just part of the culture.'

It emerged later that officers from the NSW Department of Primary Industries had attempted to catch a large bull shark near the mouth of the Richmond River just hours before Sam's attack, but that the shark refused to take the bait and swam out into the open ocean. No-one was in the water so beachgoers were not warned of the sighting. Ballina spanner-crab fisherman Cliff Corbett lamented that people were 'just blindly going into the water' regardless of the warning signs.

'We've got that many bull sharks here it's not funny and they are the nastiest, most highly testosterone-fuelled creatures on God's earth. They're snap happy,' Cliff said. 'It was that time of the year when the bull sharks are mating. If you get between them, holy fucking hell, the bull shark will arch its back and go you. They are bad news.'

Dave Pearson has intimate, first-hand knowledge of the aggressive nature of the bull shark. Dave was also making regular trips to Ballina.

'It was traumatic,' Dave said. 'Every time there was another attack, everyone in [Bite Club] copped a hiding, mentally and emotionally. I was going up there [to Ballina] to visit people, to try to provide some support. They were scared. Everybody was going into meltdown. Every time there was another attack you got angry and frustrated and hurt. You know exactly what's happening. All of us go back there: "That's my day again." We never asked to be part of this. We got dragged into it. But we're all working through it together.'

A few weeks after Sam Morgan's attack at North Wall, Dave travelled up to Ballina to take Darren Rogers surfing.

'It was just before Christmas and Darren hadn't been surfing that much at all [since Tadashi's attack] – he'd spent nearly 10 months out of the water.'

Darren had actually attempted to go surfing four times in those 10 months, but hadn't lasted longer than 15 minutes in the water. The first time, about a month after Tadashi's attack, he sought safety in numbers, joining a crowd of surfers huddled together in a tight pack at Skennars Head, about 5 kilometres north of Shelly Beach.

'I was completely freaking out,' Darren said. 'I never surf in a crowd but I went out and sat on the edge. There were still lots of [shark] sightings and there were dolphins everywhere. I couldn't last because I was just waiting to get attacked.'

Remarkably, Darren's next attempt was at Shelly Beach itself. 'I thought: "I've got to do this. I've got to go out to the spot [where Tadashi was attacked] and break through and overcome this." [The ocean] was clean and there were a couple of good waves, but there was no-one out – people had just stopped surfing on their own around here. This guy walked up to me on the beach and said: "Are you really going to do that?" I said: "Yeah, I've got to do my thing." He said: "There's heaps of guys over [at Lighthouse Beach] and there's safety in numbers." I paddled out and just got out the back when this huge bait ball surrounded me, with cormorants dive-bombing all around me. The water was black, writhing with fish, and I was right in the middle of it. I couldn't believe it. I was duck-diving through a black wall of fish and I was just waiting for a great white to come charging through. I spun around and came in. That was it. I couldn't do it.'

Then Dave Pearson arrived with fellow Bite Club members Dale Carr and Kevin Young. They took Darren surfing at Sharpes Beach near Lennox Head.

'It was great,' Dave said. 'To see [Darren] surfing again was so good. We were all out there surfing together.'

Darren felt an 'unbelievable connection' with Kevin Young, whose 19-year-old son Zac was attacked and killed by a 3-metre tiger shark while bodyboarding at The Well, north of Coffs Harbour, on 30 November 2013. The Port Macquarie teenager had only just gained his driver's licence and set off on a surf trip along the coast to Coffs with friends Kurt Gillan, Lindsy Isaac and Shayden Schrader. Like Tadashi, both of Zac's legs were bitten off in the attack. Kurt heroically paddled him in to shore and performed CPR.

'I did for someone else's son what [Kurt] did for Kevin's son,' Darren explained. 'We both know what that means. I met Tadashi's family the week after [the attack]. They came over from Japan and they wanted to know everything. It was a very difficult thing to do and very intense, but I was able to take them to the exact bit of sand where it all happened. We all kneeled down and prayed. It was a very difficult day for all of us. They were living in a horror movie and I was able to tell them what state he was in, that he wasn't screaming and crying, that he didn't suffer.

'I wish it didn't happen but I wouldn't change what I did. If I could replay that day, I would do exactly what I did. One of the biggest benefits was that I got to play a big role in his parents' understanding of the event. I had the opportunity to relieve some of their trauma and grief. That helped me a lot, too.'

A member of the evangelical Christian movement Youth for Christ, Zac Young prayed as his friends paddled desperately for the beach.

'He began to pray: "Please God, my Lord and Saviour, help protect my friends and help me through this time of need",' Kurt wrote in a tribute on Facebook. 'He passed away peacefully, no pain, with his last words to me being: "I love you brother."'

Like his son, Kevin is a committed Christian who believes Zac is 'in a better place now'.

'I love the ocean,' Kevin told *Good Weekend* magazine. 'Zac's ashes went into the ocean. His blood was spilt in the ocean. For me, Zac's essence is in the ocean. Zac is actually part of the ocean now.'

Mick Fanning believes his brother Sean's spirit is also part of the ocean. When Sean and Joel Green died, local Indigenous artist and dancer Dhinawan held a ceremony to release their spirits, which included throwing two boomerangs out into the water.

'We said if anyone found [the boomerangs] to give them to the parents,' Dhinawan explained in *Surf for Your Life*.

While Joel's boomerang was found and returned to his family, Sean's boomerang was never recovered.

'I told Mick: "Sean's spirit lives in the ocean now and you can visit him whenever you like. Any time you're out there in the ocean, your brother's spirit is out there. Take that time to be with him." You could see it helped.'

Dhinawan also told Mick that in the culture of the Gamillaroi and Bigambul tribes of southern Queensland and northern New South Wales, dolphins and whales represented visiting ancestors (similar to ancient Hawaiian culture). Almost a decade later, in November 2007, Mick was in Imbituba in southern Brazil on the cusp of a maiden world surfing title. He needed to finish ahead of the greatest competitive surfer of all time, Kelly Slater, at the Santa Catarina Pro at Imbituba's Praia da Vila to realise a lifelong dream.

'Ever since I was a little kid I've dreamt of this,' he admitted at the time. 'I don't know what's going to happen. I'm just going to go out there and do what I do, surf the best that I can, and hopefully everything goes well.'

When Mick went surfing the next day, a dolphin appeared beside him. On the final day of competition in Brazil, the dolphin appeared during each of his heats. He won them all, including the final, and was crowned champion of the world.

'I don't know if [the dolphin] was my brother or what. It was amazing. Yeah. I think it was Sean.'

Having lived through every surfer's nightmare, Mick's views about marine conservation have not so much changed, but been rattled loose. He has previously supported the direct action of marine conservation organisation Sea Shepherd, but now he's not so sure what he thinks about conservation versus cull, conscious that supporting shark culling would 'create a media shit storm'.

'What do you do?' he asked, wrestling with the shark, again. 'It's hard to say to go and kill a shark but why is it happening? I'm not going to sit here and say go and kill every shark, but if a dog bites someone, the dog gets put down. If a shark bites someone, we let it go and see what happens. If that shark keeps coming back and biting people, we should be able to do something about it, but to go and kill every shark in the ocean? No, that's just stupid.

'It should start with finding out why there's such a sudden influx. I heard rumours that they buried [dead] whales on the beach [in northern NSW]. I did some research and it's definitely happened. If the government has gone and done that, they need to fix the problem somehow. But how? The shark nets are a deterrent but they're not a hundred per cent. There's nothing that's a hundred per cent. The magnets, the shark repellents – if a great white wants you, it's going to take you. It doesn't matter what you do. We are so insignificant. Our lives are in someone else's hands right there. There's nothing you can do.'

PART FOUR

13

GONE ROGUE

THE PACIFIC SURFLINER train sped past the small Amtrak station at Surf Beach, heading south, hugging the central Californian coast towards Point Conception. The indigenous Chumash people called the distant point Humqaq, a sacred site also known as the Western Gate: a gateway for souls of the dead to begin their journey from the mortal world to the heavenly paradise of Similaqsa, where they would be reincarnated.

Beside the train line there was a sandy walking track. Beyond a fence of rusted metal and decaying cyclone wire, hummocks of sand topped with dune scrub stretched down to the water's edge. A burst of yellow sunflowers adorned the fence amid a sprawling memorial for Lucas Ransom and Francisco Solorio Jr: two victims of savage great white shark attacks at Surf Beach exactly two years and one day apart, on 22 October 2010 and 23 October 2012 respectively.

The nature and timing of the attacks fitted into a broader pattern of shark encounters at Surf Beach, which led some shark experts to suggest that Lucas and Fran were both killed by the same rogue shark: an enormous great white, at least 5 metres long, with a taste for human flesh.

The deadly pattern of shark attacks began on 8 September 2008, when local winemaker and avid surfer Kyle Knapp was knocked off his surfboard by a large great white shark. It was the first shark encounter ever reported at Surf Beach, a wild and isolated stretch of Californian coast 240 kilometres north of Los Angeles, with a history littered with more than 30 shipwrecks. (Early residents of nearby Lompoc made their houses from the scavenged wreckage of the *Sibyl Marston*, the largest steam schooner built on the west coast of the US, which ran aground at Surf Beach in 1909.) Knapp was surfing alone. It was overcast and the ocean was glassy. He was sitting on his surfboard 50 metres from shore when, at around 10.30 am, a pod of a dozen dolphins swam through the line-up. A minute later he was violently hit from behind and up-ended.

'I slid off the left side of my board as the shark pushed my board forward,' Knapp recalled in his official report.

> The shark came to the surface with my board in its mouth. It was on my right and so close to me that I could see its eye roll back in the socket as it kept pushing and biting my board. It began to thrash wildly in the water and I was struck by its tail as it descended out of sight.

Then, just over two years later, on 22 October 2010, teenage bodyboarder Lucas Ransom was mauled to death by a giant great white shark at Surf Beach. The 19-year-old chemical engineering student at the University of California's Santa Barbara campus had been tracking a storm system as it moved down the coast from Alaska. Lucas left his college dorm before dawn and paddled out in the grey, early morning light with roommate Matthew Garcia. Garcia had never been to Surf Beach before and took some time 'to get everything dialled in', while Lucas proceeded to catch four 'massive barrels'. But then, as the pair waited for a wave 100 metres from shore, a shark bit Lucas's left leg and dragged him underwater.

'It [was] just like a ninja came through and took him under,' Garcia said on *The Early Show*. As he told Surfline:

There was no sign, there was nothing. It was all very fast, very stealth. I heard something break the surface behind me and I glanced over to my right. I saw the side of a massive fish and within nanoseconds realised it was a white shark. Then I heard the bones crunch. When the shark hit [Lucas], he just said: 'Help me dude.' He knew what was going on. Then he disappeared in a cloud of red.

A huge set of waves rolled through the Surf Beach line-up, separating Garcia from his friend.

Lucas surfaced about twenty yards [away] and got sucked over the falls of a wave entirely made up of his blood. The water [at Surf Beach] is blue, as blue as it could ever be, and it was just red, the whole wave. It was an eerie sight. The wave was completely red and he was at the top of the wave.

Eventually Garcia recovered Lucas's body from the cruel sea, but the shark had ripped off his leg at the pelvis.

> He was just floating in the water. I flipped him over on his back. Right when I grabbed him he was still alive. I looked into his eyes and I saw his life end. All the blood in his body was gone. He was just kind of lifeless, just dead weight.

Then, nearly two years to the day, on 23 October 2012, local surfer Francisco Solorio Jr was attacked and killed by a monster great white shark at Surf Beach. It was almost noon when Fran and Gary Montenegro were finishing a morning surf with friends. They were sitting about 100 metres from shore, in close vicinity to the location of Lucas Ransom's deadly attack, waiting to catch a wave in.

'We had all got really good waves,' Montenegro told Discovery Channel. 'Fran had an exceptionally awesome day. Then it all happened.'

An enormous shark attacked the 39-year-old from below with ferocious speed, biting his surfboard and upper torso and dragging his body underwater. Montenegro instinctively paddled towards the churning water. Fran suddenly reappeared, desperately grasping for his surfboard and crying for help before lapsing into unconsciousness.

> He was there out of the corner of my eye and he wasn't that far from me. Basically I swam over and helped him in. [It went from] a really good day to the worst day of my life. I just figured any second I was number two. I've never been through anything close to this. Post-traumatic stress is a pretty weird thing.

Fran grew up in the nearby Santa Maria Valley and had been riding waves at Surf Beach since he was a young boy. He worked in construction, building playgrounds, and was a much-loved member of the local surfing community.

'It didn't deserve to happen,' Montenegro said. 'He was a good guy. His family … the guy did everything right.'

The youngest of five siblings, Fran left behind a wife and two young daughters. His older sister, Patricia, told the *Santa Maria Times* that the family found solace in the fact that her brother died doing what he loved.

'From the very beginning, we've had the understanding that it wasn't some beast out to get him,' Patricia said. 'It just happened. It's incredible odds, but it happened.'

Then, another two years later, on 3 October 2014, a massive 6-metre great white shark attacked sea kayaker Ryan Howell about 200 metres off the coast of Surf Beach. Ryan was fishing from his kayak with friends Brad Rudolph and Vince Culliver when the shark attacked from below, biting the kayak and launching him 5 metres into the air.

'The shark almost completely breached the water,' Culliver told KEYT-TV.

In the air the shark turned its body to the right, like an airplane banking. There was such an enormous wake that it pushed us away from Ryan and his kayak. We were yelling for Ryan because we lost sight of him in the turbulence.

Ryan was in the water, pinned to the kayak, which was being savaged by the shark.

'As soon as I hit the water my boat hit me,' he told *Kayak Fish* magazine. 'The shark was pushing it. The only thing between the shark's mouth and me was the [kayak]. It's amazing that I'm still alive.'

Four attacks in six years. Each occurring almost exactly two years apart, all very similar in nature, by the same species and at the same location: a remote and desolate beach 6 kilometres from the nearest town. It didn't take much imagination for people to wonder if it was a single rogue shark returning to the same hunting ground every second October as it migrated from the seal colonies of northern California to the warmer waters of Mexico.

Documentary filmmaker Jeff Kurr has made more than 30 TV shows about sharks, including five of the top 10 highest-rating programs screened during Discovery Channel's wildly popular Shark Week. Kurr explored the Surf Beach attacks in his 2013 documentary *Great White Serial Killer* and again in his 2015 documentary *Return of the Great White Serial Killer*. According to him, satellite tagging of female great white sharks identified a 'very precise and very accurate' two-year migration cycle, looping south from the Farallon Islands off the coast of San Francisco to Guadalupe Island, 240 kilometres off the coast of Mexico's Baja California Peninsula.

'They often return, a lot like a homing pigeon,' Kurr said.

According to Kurr, the great white shark population on America's west coast was estimated to be fewer than 500 (the great white was added to California's *Endangered Species Act* in 2013 as a result of studies that estimated the total population to be 340 adult and juvenile sharks), and only a handful grow to the size of those identified in the Surf Beach attacks.

It's a massive great white shark and a rare shark because it takes
a long time for them to grow that large. It's difficult for them to
live that long. Very few sharks reach sixteen feet [4.9 metres]
plus. The list of suspects in these attacks is very short.

If anyone could identify the list of suspects, it was veteran
shark scientist Ralph Collier. A short, pot-bellied man with
fleshy jowls and a drooping moustache, Ralph has studied shark
behaviour off the Californian coast for more than five decades –
ever since he went night fishing on Malibu Pier as an inquisitive
13-year-old and a nearby fisherman landed a spiny dogfish shark.
Ralph learned his craft under the watchful eye of legendary
California Academy of Sciences ichthyologist William Follett. He
has since investigated hundreds of great white shark attacks and
assisted the Santa Barbara Sherriff's Department with the autopsies
of both Lucas Ransom and Francisco Solorio. Ralph said that it
was notable that both incidents were violent, predatory attacks,
not investigative bites.

'In 50 years of analysing shark attacks along the Pacific Coast
these two were the most violent and vicious attacks I've ever been
involved with,' he said in *Great White Serial Killer*.

The victims were struck from below in an ambush attack or
predatory attack, when the shark attempts to kill the prey on
contact. The majority of attacks off the west coast [of North
America], better than eighty-five per cent, are investigation.

Ralph said that 'the other thing that's interesting' is that both
attacks occurred in clear water: Garcia referred to water 'as blue
as it could ever be', while several surfers reported that water visibility was so good on the day of Fran's attack that they could see

sand ripples on the ocean floor, some 4 metres below the surface. In 1996, Ralph co-authored a research paper about great white shark attacks on inanimate objects along the Pacific Coast. He does not believe that great white sharks mistake humans for their natural prey; he believes that the fatal attacks on Lucas Ransom and Francisco Solorio were not cases of mistaken identity.

That's a misconception in my opinion. As long as you have good water visibility where the shark can distinguish the object clearly, in no way do they mistake us for a pinniped [a semi-aquatic marine mammal, including seals, sea lions and walruses]. Predatory attacks are very violent, high-energy encounters. Those types of attacks are also used when the shark perceives something as a threat. An example: white sharks ram boats. Well, they're not ramming a boat because it looks like an elephant seal or a whale, because whales don't have propellers, don't make noises and don't have people moving around in them.

However, Ralph does not think a single rogue shark with a taste for human flesh was responsible for the Surf Beach attacks. He performed a forensic examination of the bite marks from both attacks and even sent tooth fragments found in Lucas's bodyboard to be sampled for DNA.

The shark's teeth are 'very distinctive,' he explained. 'There's a large space between each tooth, they are serrated and they are very sharp. When they penetrate they leave a very distinct impression.'

Examining the bite marks enabled Ralph to determine the size of the sharks involved and to make comparisons between the two attacks.

The shark that killed Lucas Ransom in October of 2010 was approximately sixteen to seventeen feet [4.8–5.2 metres] in length. The shark that killed Solorio two years later was between fifteen and sixteen feet [4.6–4.8 metres]. Sharks don't shrink as they get older. They tend to grow. These two specific attacks, I would categorically state that it would be highly unlikely that the same shark caused both attacks.

Eminent Australian surgeon Victor Coppleson coined the phrase 'rogue shark' in the 1930s. A cluster of shark attacks at Bondi Beach in 1928 and 1929 created widespread panic about a so-called 'shark menace' off Sydney's most popular stretch of sand. On Saturday 14 April 1928, 19-year-old lifesaver Maxwell Steele lost a leg after he was savagely mauled while bodysurfing just 10 metres from shore. Nine months later, on 13 January 1929, 14-year-old Colin Stewart was 'horribly mutilated' by a large shark in waist-deep water, dying in hospital from savage bites to his hip and thigh. On 8 February 1929, 39-year-old swimmer John Gibson became the second fatal shark attack victim in the space of 28 days when he was 'terribly mangled' while swimming beyond the breaking waves at Bondi, some 50 metres from dry sand. All three victims were rushed to nearby St Vincent's Hospital, where Victor Coppleson was the senior surgeon.

A tall man with 'a wonderful physique', Coppleson was an avid beachgoer and excellent swimmer. He was medical adviser to the Surf Life Saving Association of Australia and also a member of the Royal Zoological Society of New South Wales and the Australian Marine Sciences Association. While he possessed a general interest in marine science, the Bondi Beach attacks provided Coppleson with first-hand experience of the brutal consequences of human–shark encounters.

He became convinced that the pattern and frequency of attacks suggested the likelihood of a single shark ignoring its natural prey and acquiring a taste for human flesh. Coppleson was the Australian correspondent for UK medical journal *The Lancet* and began writing about the subject, beginning with an article in *The Medical Journal of Australia* in 1933 and culminating with the publication of his influential book *Shark Attack* in 1958. He explained:

A rogue shark, if the theory is correct, and the evidence appears to prove it to the hilt, like the man-eating tiger, is a killer which, having experienced the deadly game sport of killing or mauling a human, goes in search of similar game.

The continued presence of man-eating sharks, the attacks in sequence and cessation of attacks once a particular shark is caught, suggests the guilt, not of many sharks, but of one shark. It suggests the presence of a vicious shark which patrols a certain area of the coast, of a river or of a harbour, for long periods.

Many of Coppleson's shark theories, like his hypothesis that sharks did not attack humans in water cooler than 21°C, were later disproven by scientific evidence. However, his 'rogue shark' theory became widely accepted by the general public, in no small part due to the depiction of the bloodthirsty monster in *Jaws* and echoed most recently in the 2016 Hollywood blockbuster *The Shallows*.

'We haven't been able to shake it,' California State University shark expert Dr Chris Lowe told *Smithsonian* magazine. 'For example, in *Jaws*, they say the shark has set up a territory and it's going to stay as long as there are people to eat. No shark species has been found to exhibit territoriality [and] there's just no good evidence that the same shark has been involved on multiple attacks on people over time.'

There may well be no robust scientific evidence, but there are plenty of clusters of multiple shark attacks concentrated on specific locations that give Coppleson's theory credibility.

The horrific real-life incidents that Peter Benchley and Steven Spielberg referenced in *Jaws* were the infamous Jersey Shore attacks of July 1916, when five people were attacked – four of whom were killed – in the space of 12 days at the height of a lethal summer heatwave.

'It happened before,' Amity Island police chief Martin Brody warned in *Jaws*. 'The Jersey beach. 1916. Five people chewed up in the surf.'

This series of violent, unexpected shark attacks prompted a wave of panic, inflamed by sensationalist media reports, which ensured the vicious 'Matawan man-eater' would become part of American folklore. However, it had drifted into the collective subconscious when, almost 60 years later, *Jaws* picked the scab.

'The 1916 Jersey Shore attacks probably did more to demonize the shark in the eyes of human beings than any other single event,' historian Sean Munger said on his blog. 'One shark being responsible for all these deaths is an irresistible story, which is why Peter Benchley took the 1916 attacks as inspiration for *Jaws*.'

The attacks began on 1 July 1916, with the eastern seaboard of the US sweltering through a record heatwave. The grand hotels dotted along the Jersey Shore were full to bursting with the wealthy residents of Philadelphia and New York.

Among them was 25-year-old Charles Vansant, the son of a prominent Philadelphia doctor on holiday with his family at the ornate Engleside Hotel in Beach Haven, at the southern end of Long Beach Island. A strong and confident swimmer, Vansant went for a quick dip before dinner. A large shaggy dog followed him into the water but, as they both swam back towards the beach, a shark grasped Vansant's left leg and refused to let go. Lifeguard Alexander Ott and several bystanders wrestled Vansant's body back to shore in a brutal tug-of-war. The shark eventually loosened its grip and Vansant was carried back to the hotel, where his father tried desperately to stem the bleeding. But much of Vansant's leg was missing, the femoral artery severed, and he bled to death on the hotel manager's desk.

People were dumbfounded. There had never been a documented shark attack in US waters. *The New York Times* headline read, 'Dies After Attack by Fish'. Some shark sceptics even suggested Vansant had been attacked by a sea turtle with 'a vicious disposition'.

Then, on 6 July 1916, 27-year-old Charles Bruder was attacked while swimming 120 metres from shore at Spring Lake, 72 kilometres north of Beach Haven. People on the beach saw a large splash and the water turn red – one woman reportedly yelled out: 'The man in the red canoe has upset.' There was no canoe. Lifeguards paddled out in a rowboat to rescue Bruder. Both his legs had been bitten off and his torso gnawed but, remarkably, the hotel bellhop was still conscious.

'He was a big grey fellow and as rough as sandpaper,' Bruder, according to reports at the time, told his rescuers before bleeding to death as he lay sprawled in the bottom of the boat.

The second fatal attack in the space of six days inspired a very different reaction. *The New York Times* headline read, 'Shark Kills Bather Off Jersey Beach'. Although the American Museum of Natural History ichthyologist John Treadwell Nichols suggested the perpetrator was a killer whale, the shark panic had set in – New Jersey beaches were closed, hotels emptied, nets installed and motorboats patrolled the shoreline.

Six days later, on 12 July 1916, retired sea captain Thomas Cottrell spotted a 2.4-metre shark in the Matawan Creek, a shallow, brackish tidal inlet 48 kilometres north of Spring Lake. Cottrell tried to raise the alarm but was either ignored or doubted. The story seemed implausible: a shark sighting 24 kilometres upriver in barely a metre of water. Later that day, 11-year-old Lester Stilwell was attacked and dragged underwater while playing with friends in a popular Matawan swimming hole. One of the boys described Lester 'being shaken like a cat shakes a mouse'. The boys had been skinny-dipping and they ran for help naked and covered in mud, screaming: 'Shark! Shark!'

Watson Stanley Fisher closed his tailor shop to join the search for Lester's body. Chicken wire was strung out across the creek and a rowboat launched. After half an hour trawling the muddy water, Fisher dove down and dragged the boy's lifeless body to the surface. Almost immediately, the shark attacked the 24-year-old tailor, biting his right thigh, stripping the flesh from groin to kneecap. Fisher reached the shore and was rushed by train to hospital, where he died from blood loss.

About half an hour after Fisher's attack, barely a kilometre downriver, 12-year-old Joseph Dunn was attacked while swimming at a bend in Matawan Creek. Dunn was climbing out of the water on a ladder when a shark latched onto his left leg, dragging him back into the water. His brother Michael pulled him free and doctors later saved his badly mangled leg.

The response was swift and brutal. The mayor of Matawan printed 'wanted' posters offering a $100 reward to anyone who killed a shark in the creek. President Woodrow Wilson called a cabinet meeting at the White House and the cabinet agreed to provide public money to 'drive away all the ferocious man-eating sharks which have been making prey of bathers'. *The New York Times* reported on 'the score of men who went out to hunt [sharks] with rifles, shotguns, boat hooks, harpoons, pikes and dynamite'.

Among them was 40-year-old former Barnum & Bailey lion tamer and big game hunter–cum–taxidermist Michael Schleisser. On 14 July 1916, Schleisser dramatically beat a 2.3-metre juvenile great white shark to death with a broken oar in Raritan Bay, just off the coast of South Amboy and less than 10 kilometres from the mouth of Matawan Creek. When Schleisser gutted his catch, he removed 'suspicious fleshy material and bones' that filled 'about two-thirds of a milk crate' according to *Bronx News*. Schleisser mounted the shark and placed it on display in the window of his taxidermy shop in Harlem, New York. The esteemed Dr Frederic Lucas, director of the nearby American Museum of Natural History, inspected the shark and identified the remains found within it as human, including a shin bone and a rib.

However, it seemed highly unlikely that Schleisser's shark was responsible for all five attacks, if any. The great white shark is an oceanic species that cannot survive in fresh water. Juvenile great whites feed mainly on fish: their jaws of layered mineralised cartilage are not yet strong enough to tackle marine mammals like seals, let alone humans. In fact, Dr Lucas believed that the human remains came from a body that had been dead for some time, possibly a drowning victim, while others accused Schleisser of planting the bones himself. In *The Book of Sharks*, American naturalist Richard Ellis suggested that the Matawan Creek attacks in particular were perpetrated by one or several bull sharks, which are known to frequent shallow, brackish water.

'To try to make the facts as we know them conform to the "rogue shark" theory is stretching sensationalism and credibility beyond reasonable limits,' Ellis wrote in *The Book of Sharks*.

Yet as soon as Schleisser caught his shark, the Jersey Shore attacks abruptly stopped, just as Coppleson had theorised.

There has only been one suspected fatal shark attack in New Jersey since Stanley Fisher was mauled in Matawan Creek in 1916. In contrast, there have been 14 fatal shark attacks off the Californian coast since 1952, including the two violent attacks at Surf Beach. Every October, the family and friends of Lucas Ransom and Francisco Solorio return to the rugged stretch of Californian coast to remember their loved ones. The families first met on the one-year anniversary of Fran's death.

'We know the pain that they're going through,' Lucas's mum, Candace, told the *Santa Barbara News*.

Something that horrific, that is so incredible, you don't believe something like that has ever happened. It's so rare that it does happen. We have gone through an experience few people ever do. I'm so grateful to have the opportunity to meet with them, so we can continue to honour their memories.

The families have built rambling memorials for Luke and Fran alongside the railway line – large rocks painted with their names, decorated with shells, matchbox cars and a plastic toy whale. Wooden crosses and Buddha statues rest atop the dunes. The initials 'LR' and 'FS' have been spray-painted on the metal fence, which has been festooned with bright yellow flowers.

Fran's sister Patricia told the *Santa Maria Times* that she hopes that the memorials serve as a warning to other surfers who continue to frequent the dangerous waters off Surf Beach.

I wish that people wouldn't take it so lightly. It's very obvious something's going on out here. I'm not saying don't go in the water. I'm saying maybe not here, maybe not in October. It's not just about a decision they make to go surfing. There's families, children.

She said that Fran's eldest daughter still spoke to her father. 'She talks about Daddy being up in the sun.'

14

AFRAID OF
THE SHARK

PSYCHOLOGISTS AND SHARK experts almost universally
agree that sensationalist media reports (like those surrounding the two fatal attacks in Western Australia in June 2016,
when the front page of *The West Australian* displayed a large
Photoshopped dorsal fin behind two children playing in the
ocean) have combined with negative portrayals in films like *Jaws*
and a general lack of understanding about the species to create an
irrational and unjustified fear of sharks. The cliché is that you are
more likely to be killed by a bee sting, falling coconut, lightning
strike or vending machine.

Dr Frank Gaskill is a psychologist from North Carolina who
specialises in Asperger syndrome. Ever since he watched *Jaws* as
a seven-year-old, Frank has been terrified of sharks.

'I think about sharks every single time I go in the water,' he
confessed to psychology website Shrink Tank.

Frank suggested that his fear of sharks could be best explained by the following equation: Availability Heuristic + Emotions + Method of Death − Logic = Fear of Sharks.

'Availability heuristic' is a psychological term for when we make decisions based on what immediately comes to mind. Put simply, it is a mental shortcut that enables us to make decisions quickly, without in-depth investigation, relying on the first thing that pops into our brain.

> To remember watching Quint die a horrible death from *Jaws* is more readily accessed by the brain than the logical fact that you have one in three million odds of being bitten by a shark. The brain sees the more easily recalled information as more important but is devoid of logic.

The next factor in Frank's equation is the role of emotions. Decision-making, once considered a process of rational think-ing, is, most psychologists now agree, predominantly driven by emotion. Every day, we make decisions to avoid negative feelings like guilt and anxiety, or to increase positive feelings like happi-ness and pride. These positive and negative emotional states have been described as biologically evolved traits.

In his 1872 book *The Expression of the Emotions in Man and Animals*, Charles Darwin linked emotional states to actions, concluding that emotions enabled humans and animals to act quickly to ensure survival. In 1915, Harvard physiologist Walter Bradford Cannon coined the phrase 'fight or flight' to describe an animal's response to a threatening situation. Cannon and colleague Philip Bard then developed a theory of emotion that detailed the neurological process of how emotions informed physical reactions. The example commonly used to explain the theory was the sighting of a bear in the woods, which would immediately trigger a subjective feeling of fear, resulting in physiological changes like rapid heartbeat, heavy breathing, sweating and adrenaline, consistent with 'fight or flight'.

'Seaside villagers two thousand years ago didn't have stats on shark attacks,' Frank said.

But if one of their buddies got chewed up while on a swim, I guarantee he's not thinking of the two thousand people in his village who were never attacked. He's making decisions based on seeing that blood in the water.

Next comes method of death. The primal fear of being eaten alive is another evolutionary hangover of our ancestors having been prey.

'Fear is adaptive because it protects us,' behavioural and cognitive therapist Dr Robert Leahy told *Psychology Today*. 'More importantly, it protected our ancestors. It is natural to be afraid of many of the things that we are afraid of.'

Humans are hardwired to be afraid of being eaten, yet in the developed world encounters with wild predators are incredibly rare. The one notable exception is in the ocean, where an average of six people were killed by shark bites each year from 2005 to 2015.

In 1916, at the time of the Jersey Shore attacks, 'sea bathing' was a relatively new phenomenon, while swimming in the ocean during daylight hours was actually banned in Australia until 1902.

The spread of seaside resorts, increase in leisure time, availability of modern transport, boom in mass tourism and popularity of swimming and other water-based activities have all combined to make the beach an attractive and romantic destination: 68 per cent of respondents to a recent TripAdvisor survey identified the beach as the perfect place to honeymoon. Beachside holidays are rooted in a tradition of journeying from the city to the countryside that dates back to the industrial revolution and growth of urban populations in the eighteenth century. The beach has become a space for physical, mental and spiritual respite from the fast-paced modern world, but it is also an unpredictable borderland to the natural world.

'It's where the land meets the sea, where civilisation meets the wild,' American surf writer Drew Kampion explained in surf film *Uncharted Waters*. 'You're going back and forth from a world where you might be eaten or drowned, and a world where you can have a hot dog.'

The real kicker is that there is little evidence that sharks eat humans. The term 'man-eater' is actually a misnomer, according to California State University shark expert Dr Chris Lowe.

'Most people that are attacked are bitten but they are rarely consumed,' Dr Lowe said in a lecture at the Aquarium of the Pacific in Long Beach, California.

> In fact, most people are bitten and the shark swims away. I've interviewed surfers who have been bitten by sharks and who are hundreds of yards offshore, they're bleeding profusely, and they tell me: 'I out-paddled the shark to the beach.' I hate to tell them, but if the shark was intent on eating them, they would've never have made it to the beach … They would never be able to outswim a shark. So the reality of it is that the shark may have bitten them, but it obviously didn't have any intent on eating them.

Dr Lowe suggested that one reason sharks don't eat humans is that we are not fat enough. He explained how scientists using slaughtered sheep to attract great white sharks to the surface in the waters off the Farallon Islands found that sharks would only eat pregnant sheep, which have a higher fat content.

> White sharks … are actually kind of picky. They wouldn't eat the scrawny sheep [and] white sharks would much prefer to eat an elephant seal, which has a higher fat content, than a sea lion … If you compare our fat content to that of a marine mammal, most pinnipeds can have up to fifty per cent body fat, [while] most humans are around sixteen per cent body fat, and some of the really athletic ones are down around four per cent body fat … Maybe that's why surfers get bitten and spit out – they're not fat enough.

Which brings us to the final variable in Frank's equation: logic. A word that comes from the Ancient Greeks, logic is the study of one or more arguments and assumptions to find a conclusive truth. Dr Frank Gaskill suggested that his fear of sharks was devoid of logic partly because he didn't know or understand all the scientific and evidence-based arguments needed to form a conclusive truth. The public perception of sharks, particularly the large, oceanic species like the great white and tiger shark, has undoubtedly been shaped by the way the media and popular culture have portrayed them, from *Jaws* to *The Shallows*, from Discovery Channel's Shark Week to the cult *Sharknado* series.

'They are a top level predator, they get very large and they can be scary,' Dr Lowe said.

A lot of people have viewed sharks as something bad … because they're dangerous and scary. The problem is that because of that reputation, we've struggled in the scientific community to provide the public with good, solid information about these animals. Shark Week is probably some of the most popular public broadcasting on the planet … Unfortunately, only about forty per cent of what you're hearing in Shark Week is actually factual … there's not a lot of good science or evidence to back up a lot of the supposed facts that they put out to the public.

Dr Lowe is a professor in marine biology and director of the Shark Lab at California State University, which was established more than 50 years ago to study the biology and behaviour of sharks. Tall and lean with a long, expressive face and a goatee, Chris grew up fishing and diving the waters around Martha's Vineyard off the Massachusetts coast, where *Jaws* was filmed, and comes from a long line of New England fishermen and whalers. Nowadays, he is at the forefront of great white shark research. There would be very few, if any, people on the planet who know more about the great white shark than Dr Chris Lowe, yet even Chris has more questions than answers about this most notorious of shark species.

His biggest question is why great white sharks bite people. 'The thing that keeps me scratching my head is: "Why would a shark waste the energy and potentially injure itself biting something … but not eat it? Why do that?"'

Chris does not think it is because they identify humans as prey ('If we look at shark attack records, typically the most populated beaches on the planet experience the least number of shark attacks'), or that they mistake humans for their natural prey.

'[They] might actually do it as a defence. We think of sharks as being these ultimate predators, but they can also be prey.'

For example, killer whales (*Orcinus orca*) have been witnessed attacking and killing great white sharks near the Neptune Islands in South Australia and the Farallon Islands in California, working together to lift the shark out of the water, causing it to suffocate and die, then eating the dead shark's liver.

It's possible that sharks may bite people [because] they consider us a threat. We know that during mating season, there is some evidence that sharks display some warning behaviour to ward off potential [rivals] and potential predators. So imagine if you've got a surfer sitting on the water ... The shark's down there going: 'You're in my space.' And it's doing its whole thing. But the surfer can't see underwater ... Even if he could, could he interpret the behaviour? Probably not. But the shark is going: 'Okay, I warned you.' Boom. It takes a bite and then it flees.

15

I'VE BEEN BIT

THE GREAT FISH was stalking the coastline from Mānā Point to Majors Bay on the westernmost edge of the Hawaiian island of Kauai. It had been raining for days. Turbid clouds of muddy water stained the turquoise bay, washing it with overflow from the island's steep volcanic mountains, vast canyons, corn plantations and a nearby shrimp farm. The nutrient-rich concoction, concentrated at the mouth of the Waieli Drain, lured marine life closer to shore.

Overhead waves peaked on a shallow sandbar further south, where 18-year-old bodyboarder Mike Coots was surfing with a group of friends, oblivious to the shark circling the line-up with increasingly manic intensity. Mike paddled for a wave, splashing and kicking on the surface. The shark surged up from the murky depths. Boom. It bit down on Mike's right leg, lifting his body up out of the water and shaking him violently from side to side, like 'a dog with a piece of meat'.

'It was so fast,' Mike said. 'I didn't see it coming. There was no splashing. I didn't see a fin. I was completely blindsided. It literally came up from straight underneath me like a submarine and grabbed onto me. As soon as it was out of the water and locked on to my leg, it was obvious that I was getting attacked by a shark. I knew exactly what was happening. It was a kind of surreal, out-of-body experience to be honest. It felt like it wasn't really happening to me: I was just going along with the motions. It sort of did this ragdoll back and forth, shaking its head, kind of like a pit bull. Things were happening so quickly but it felt like a slowed down movie. I remember swaying back and forth. I wasn't scared. I got this really creepy feeling.'

Lean and angular with a friendly, all-American face, Mike leaned forward with furrowed brow. His voice dropped a decibel.

'It was an incredibly creepy, spooked out, get-away-from-me feeling,' he said. 'We have centipedes here in Hawaii and when you see them you kind of get chicken skin and the hairs on your arms stand up. Or like when you're home alone and you hear a noise in the garage and instinctively you're on high alert. One hundred per cent I had that exact feeling. I knew I just had to get away from the situation. At first I stuck my right hand in its mouth. It had my leg and I stuck my hand in its jaws to try to get my leg out. That didn't work. I cut my finger pretty bad. After I did that it started opening its mouth a little bit, trying to get a better grip. I just remember feeling this immense pressure compressing my legs. There was no pain, just a lot of pressure. Instinctively, I punched it with my left hand. I cracked it above the nose, maybe two or three times. That was totally instinct:

fight or flight. As soon as I hit it on the nose it let go, released its grip on my leg, and disappeared back underwater.'

The entire encounter was over in a matter of seconds. Mike got back on his bodyboard and started paddling for shore. But he soon realised that his finger was badly damaged. 'It was split open like a potato. I could see the bone and everything. There was a guy right next to me. He must have been only five feet away from me when I got attacked. He just had this pale, freaked out look on his face. I didn't know what to do or what to tell him. I just yelled: "Shark! Go in!" He started paddling in and I paddled in behind him. Then my right leg started doing this weird spasm. I remember thinking: "Oh no, the shark is grabbing me again." I looked back over my shoulder expecting to see jaws just attacking me but all I saw was my leg missing, sticking out of the water, perfectly severed. A surgeon couldn't have done a better job. Then it just hit me: "I've been bit." I had no idea I was even hurt, but my leg was gone.'

A wave washed Mike into the shallows. He tried to stand up but fell over, rolling on the shoreline like a crumbed cutlet covered in blood and sand. Mike's friend, professional bodyboarder Kyle Maligro, rushed to his aid, wrapping a bodyboard leash around Mike's thigh to act as a makeshift tourniquet. (Orthopedic surgeon Thomas Grollman later credited Kyle's quick thinking for saving Mike's life.) Mike was then loaded onto the bed of local surfer Keith Karasic's pick-up truck and rushed to the ER at Kauai Veterans Memorial Hospital.

'I remember flying down the road to the hospital lying down in the bed of the truck with blood just pouring out of my leg and down through the tailgate. I got attacked pretty early in the morning, around the same time kids were getting to school, and I remember passing all these cars full of parents and kids. As we passed them, they would look at me in the bed of the truck with my foot torn off and they would just pull over. I'll never forget the look on their face when they realised what was going on.'

Mike was unconscious when he arrived at the small 45-bed hospital. He was stabilised and transferred to the largest of Kauai's three hospitals, Wilcox Medical Center in Lihue, where he underwent emergency surgery and remained in an induced coma for almost two days. 'I woke up and my family and friends were all there. I kind of thought I wasn't going to make it and, maybe it was the morphine, but I just felt grateful to have survived; that I was there and my family was there and life was good. But everyone had this kind of freaked out look. My mum said: "You know you lost your leg?" I was like: "Duh!"'

Mike Coots is not your average house cat. Mike was fresh out of high school when the tiger shark attacked him on Kauai's west coast on 28 October 1997, biting off his right leg. Two months after the attack, the junior bodyboarding champion was back in the ocean, paddling out at the very same stretch of beach.

'It was Mother Nature,' Mike explained. 'It was actually pretty close to where I got bit, but the only reason was because the surf happened to be good there on the day I was ready to go back in the ocean. I wasn't trying to jump back on the horse right where the horse bucked me off. That was just the best spot that day. I remember going down to the water's edge with my crutches. I remember jumping in the ocean and it felt glorious. I grew up in the ocean. That was really all I knew. Island life is diving, swimming and surfing. Sharks are just part of the environment. I carry no animosity towards the shark. How can you really get mad at something for doing what it's done for hundreds of millions of years? If I was a tourist visiting Kauai and I had jumped in the water on the first day of my vacation and the shark had attacked me – that would be a little different. But I grew up in the ocean. It just goes with the territory. The hardest part of the whole ordeal was being out of the water.'

While Mike was out of the water he began playing with cameras, initially filming friends surfing. Then professional photographer John Russell visited Kauai to shoot a portrait of Mike for a magazine feature. Russell returned a few months later for a *Sports Illustrated* shoot and hired Mike as his assistant.

'I was trying to figure out what I was going to do now that my bodyboarding career was over,' Mike said. 'I thought I'd like to do this as a living.'

Mike enrolled in a Bachelor of Fine Arts in Professional Photography at the Brooks Institute in Santa Barbara, California. Six months after the attack, he had been fitted with a prosthetic. California's long, flat waves were not suited to bodyboarding, so Mike decided to try stand-up surfing. 'The mellow point breaks there were much better suited for stand-up surfing. I remember that first surf clearly. I was told by my prosthetist not to take my prosthetic leg in the water; it would void the warranty, rust, and could even fall off. I kept touching the foot and socket to make sure it wasn't disintegrating like the Wicked Witch of the West and it wasn't seizing up like the Tin Man. It took about ten minutes or so checking and rechecking the leg before my confidence kicked in enough to catch a wave. A very, very tiny one drifted in. I caught it, awkwardly popped up, and I was surfing!'

This was in the days before GoPro cameras and selfie sticks. Mike knew he was breaking new ground: he had rigged up a board mount with insulation pipe and u-bolts from the local hardware store to hold a point-and-shoot Canon digital camera to capture his first stand-up surf. The images were remarkable and have become even more so ever since, capturing Mike's evolution both as a surfer and as a photographer.

His most recent images from Fiji are captured from deep inside the tube, from a GoPro camera mounted on the tail of his surfboard. Mike is crouched low with his hand gripping the outside rail, his metal and carbon fibre prosthetic pressed flat to the board, with the lip of the wave curving overhead: a turquoise cavern glittering in the sunshine. It is breathtaking and a vivid illustration of why Mike has more than 100,000 followers on Instagram and takes photos for *The Wall Street Journal*, *The New York Times* and *Forbes* magazine, as well as corporate clients like Four Seasons, Red Bull, H&M and Sony.

'I don't know that I'd be a professional photographer today if it wasn't for the attack,' he confessed.

Mike has found the silver lining in his shark attack.

'Stuff happens to everybody,' he said. 'It's just how we react to it that determines who we are. I don't really regret paddling out that day, or getting bitten by a shark and losing a limb. It's brought me a lot of opportunities and adventures, new relationships with people I would never have met otherwise. In a way I feel fortunate. I don't have bad dreams or hard feelings. I have come to terms with it: that I was in the wrong place at the wrong time. [Sharks] just do what they do.'

Mike doesn't see himself as a victim. He describes himself as a survivor. 'There's been a couple of rough patches with prosthetics breaking and getting blisters early on in the process of being an amputee, but otherwise it's just been a little life change and it's generally been a life change for the better.

'Early on you think you can't do this, you can't do that: there's these physical limitations on life. [But] you build up these little things, day to day, and after a while you're like: "Bring it on." What can happen that I can't figure out what to do? [Surfing with a prosthetic] was a little hard at first, but I got the hang of it. It is uncharted territory. Every time I paddle out it feels brand new. There's a lot to be learned and it is an exciting time with prosthetics. I have a little wrench and I can adjust the toe angle a little bit. I have a notebook, so I take notes. I have my GoPro camera, so I'll look at the video footage. Everything works really well going right but then you go backside, you go left, and it doesn't work so well … There are so many variables, which makes it so much fun. Then you get a good wave and you have total control of the board and you kick off at the end and think: "Whoa, everything came together." It feels really good. The ocean is pretty much my everything. It is my work, it's my passion, it's my exercise, it's my healing and sometimes it's my breadbox or my ice cooler for dinner. The ocean has taken a little bit from me but it's given me so much more.'

On 31 October 2003, almost exactly six years after Mike lost his leg, a tiger shark attacked 13-year-old Bethany Hamilton at Tunnels Beach, a popular surf spot near her family home in Hanalei, on the north shore of Kauai. Bethany was surfing with her best friend, Alana Blanchard, and Alana's dad, Holt, and 16-year-old brother, Byron. The waves were small and inconsistent. Bethany floated on the western edge of the reef, less than

5 metres from Alana, waiting patiently for a wave. Her left arm was dangling in the water.

'The shark came up and grabbed a hold of my arm,' Bethany said. 'It was like pulling me back and forth. Not like pulling me underwater, just like, you know how you eat a piece of steak? It was kind of like that. There was no pain at the time. I felt a lot of pressure and a couple of lightning-fast tugs. And then it let go. And then went under. It was over in a few seconds.'

It took Bethany a moment to realise that the shark had bitten off her arm.

'I remember seeing the water around me turn bright red with blood,' she recalled in her 2006 memoir, *Soul Surfer*. 'My left arm was gone almost to the armpit, along with a huge, crescent-shaped chunk of my surfboard.'

Bethany didn't scream or cry out. She turned to Alana and said matter-of-factly: 'I just got attacked by a shark.' Holt Blanchard took charge, taking off his Lycra rash vest and wrapping it tightly around Bethany's shoulder to stem the bleeding. He then helped her paddle to shore while Byron raced ahead and dialled 911. A devout Christian, Bethany told American broadcaster ABC that she immediately began praying to God to rescue her. 'I wasn't freaking out but I was praying to God to help me. I was praying: "Please God, let me get to the beach." And then I had this one pretty funny thought. I was thinking: "I wonder if I'm going to lose my sponsor."'

Bethany's sponsor was Australian surfing company Rip Curl. The skinny tween with stringy, sun-bleached hair was one of Hawaii's most promising young surfers. She was the top-ranked female junior surfer on Kauai and had consistently beaten much older surfers in amateur Hawaiian competitions. In fact, only five months earlier, Bethany had finished runner-up in the open women's division of the National Scholastic Surfing Association (NSSA) national championships at San Clemente, California. Now she was unconscious, being rushed to Wilcox Medical Center, having lost almost 60 per cent of the blood in her body. It was early in the morning on Halloween and Mike Coots heard the ambulance sirens screaming along Kuhio Highway.

His phone rang. It was Bethany's brother, Noah, who had gone to Kapaa High School with Mike. 'He said: "My sister just got attacked and I don't know if she's going to make it. We're going to the hospital right now. If you can, say a prayer for her." He was in hysterics. He was crying and really emotional. I hung up the phone and went straight to the hospital.'

By the time Mike arrived at the hospital, Bethany was being operated on by Dr Ken Pierce, the same emergency doctor who had amputated Mike's lower leg. 'When she came to in the hospital, right out of surgery, she opened her eyes and I was right there: the first person she saw as she came out of surgery. I'll never forget that look. It was a surreal feeling, but I knew she was going to be okay. I could tell she was going to do good things in her life. She wasn't at all upset or sad or mad or emotional. She was just like: "This is it. It is what it is. Let's move on."

'We have a special bond. We've both spent our entire lives in the ocean. The physical injuries, with the staples and stitches, were the longest period both of us had ever been out of the water. We were both itching to get back in and get wet. You just want to get back in the water.'

Bethany Hamilton was back in the water 26 days after her attack. On the day before Thanksgiving, 2003, she walked back into the surf alongside her best friend, Alana Blanchard, just as she had on that Halloween morning. This time she was on a nine-foot longboard and paddling jerkily through the broken whitewater with one arm.

'Not being able to surf, I don't know … maybe it went through my mind once, but I tried not to dwell on it,' Bethany said. 'I was not afraid of being attacked by a shark. I didn't even think about it. My whole mind was concentrated on catching a wave and getting to my feet. I struggled on my first two times and then I got up on my third wave and rode it all the way in. It was so exciting and I just had like tears of joy and I had that stoke. Even though it wasn't a good wave, it was exciting for me. Then, it just went up from there.'

Seven months later, Bethany made the final of the open women's division of the NSSA's national championships at San Clemente. She finished in fifth place but the winner, fellow Hawaiian Carissa Moore, gave Bethany her first-place trophy.

'I look up to Bethany,' Carissa told the NSSA website. 'She's one of my best friends and the way she lives her life and goes about things is really inspiring.'

The next year, in 2005, Bethany won NSSA's explorer women's division. In 2008, she finished runner-up at the World Junior Championships at North Narrabeen in Sydney.

'Adapting to surfing with one arm, I just basically set my mind to it and I think that's what really got me through a lot of it – making it my goal just to surf again,' she said. 'The hardest thing was probably just learning how to stand up … positioning yourself in the right place and learning how to catch waves in a different way. It was all pretty hard.'

Bethany did not fulfil her childhood dream of becoming a full-time competitor on surfing's elite World Championship Tour.

Instead, she set about conquering some of the world's most challenging waves. In 2014, Bethany won the Women's Pipeline Pro at the notorious Banzai Pipeline on the Hawaiian island of Oahu. In 2016, she was a finalist in the XXL Big Wave Awards for riding a gigantic wave at Pe'ahi – the Everest of big-wave surfing, more commonly known as Jaws – on the island of Maui. A few months later she defeated the number one ranked surfer in the world, Australia's Tyler Wright, to reach the semifinals of the 2016 Fiji Women's Pro at Cloudbreak, a powerful and shallow reef break off the coast of Fiji's main island, Viti Levu. Bethany's fearless performance stunned the sporting world.

'She's the greatest human probably ever,' Wright told the World Surf League website.

The other person who Noah Hamilton had called as the ambulance raced Bethany to hospital was Sarah Hill, the leader of the Kauai Christian Fellowship youth group. Bethany's faith has played a central role in her recovery. In the days after the attack, Sarah recited a passage which was drawn from the Old Testament, Jeremiah 29:11: '"For I know the plans I have for you," says the Lord, "plans of peace and not of evil, to give you a future and a hope."'

The short passage became Bethany's mantra and she became convinced that God had 'a plan and a hope' for her future.

'I think the reason I haven't gotten all bummed out about losing an arm is due to God,' she explained in *Soul Surfer*.

I think the reason I have been able to tell my story on TV and in magazines is because God wanted other people to know. I think this was God's plan for me all along. I am not saying that God made the shark bite me. I think He knew it would happen and He made a way for my life to be happy and meaningful in spite of it happening. And I am thankful. I could have died. I could have been hurt so bad that I might not have been able to surf again. I have lots and lots of things to be thankful for.

Right now, the thing that Bethany is most thankful for is her family. She married husband Adam Dirks in 2013 and gave birth to their first child, Tobias, in 2015.

'I'm so excited to tell my son about my accident, as he will see how I'm not your typical mum,' she told the UK's *Daily Mail*.

I want to show him a shark might have bitten off my arm, but that doesn't stop you in life, it just makes you even more determined and stronger. I hope my journey encourages him to follow his own dreams. I might have lost an arm, but I really have gained so, so much. I have a wonderful husband and a son and a magical career. That is a lot of blessings to be thankful for.

Mike also thinks his shark attack was a blessing in disguise.

'I recently told somebody that getting attacked by a shark was the greatest thing that's ever happened to me,' Mike said. 'They were like: "That's absurd. Why would you say that?" [But] I think it's really made me who I am today.'

Today, Mike is an active shark conservationist and spokesperson for Pew Charitable Trusts, a global research and public policy organisation based in Philadelphia that works with governments and scientists around the world to protect and conserve ocean environments, among other initiatives. 'I nearly lost my life to a shark but I really believe that sharks are one of if not the most important species in our marine ecosystem. I've learnt the science behind it all. You can't argue that, with sharks being top of the food chain, they don't play a huge role in the make-up and diversity of sea life below. If you remove them the network underneath will start to crumble. At the rate that [sharks] are being killed off, they're not going to be around in fifteen or twenty years. That will be catastrophic for ocean environments.'

In contrast to the emotional arguments for shark culls on Réunion and in Australia, Mike's measured response is reflective of a broader acceptance of sharks as an intrinsic part of the natural environment of the Hawaiian Islands. Traditional Polynesian culture has a belief system described by anthropologists as animistic or pre-animistic. Certain objects, places and people contain a spiritual energy called *mana*. Sharks contain powerful *mana*, particularly the tiger shark (*niuhi*).

In contrast with the irrational fear of sharks described by Dr Frank Gaskill, ancient Hawaiians worshipped sharks as gods and identified them as ancestral spirits. Hawaiian chiefs believed that they could see the future by eating the eyes of the *niuhi*.

The slow decline of traditional Hawaiian culture began when Captain James Cook 'discovered' the Hawaiian Islands in 1778, making landfall at Waimea Bay on Kauai's west coast. Calvinist missionaries from Boston followed, establishing a mission on Kauai in 1820. By the 1970s, the island was awash with hippies seeking refuge from the outside world, and the Vietnam War in particular.

Today, Kauai is an amalgam of its parts. There has been a Polynesian cultural renaissance, yet Kauai remains a hotbed for

Christian missions (both Sarah Hill and Adam Dirks arrived on the island as youth missionaries) with more than 100 churches for a population of around 65,000 people. There are churches of every colour and creed, but most are non-denominational and flavour religious scripture with strong pacifist and environmental themes courtesy of the island's free-loving hippie heritage.

So when a tiger shark bit off Bethany Hamilton's left arm in October 2003, the tight-knit island community's focus was on her recovery, not retribution.

'She's this really cute, bright girl who didn't deserve something like this,' Kauai-raised professional surfer Rochelle Ballard told *The Honolulu Advertiser*. 'The thing to remember is that she is a great surfer, not was. Her potential is still there.'

Unlike Réunion, Second Beach in South Africa and Ballina, Kauai was not subject to a violent cluster of shark attacks. There has not been a fatal shark attack recorded on Kauai since 24 May 1981, when spearfisher Roger Garletts disappeared at Haena Beach.

'We did hear stories about certain spots where sharks were seen or somebody got bumped,' Mike said. 'But it was not common.'

Bethany was the fourth person to lose a limb in a shark bite on Kauai since 18 October 1985, when a shark tore off bodyboarder Joe Thomson's right forearm. Bethany's attack attracted widespread media coverage, but it wasn't until after numerous sightings of a large tiger shark in Hanalei Bay that veteran local surfers and fishermen Bill Hamilton (no relation) and Ralph Young set three baited hooks inside the large half-moon bay, only a few kilometres east of Tunnels Beach. Fourteen days after Bethany's attack, they hauled a 4-metre tiger shark from the depths of the bay, which outraged the island's indigenous Hawaiian population.

'We don't hunt sharks except for large predators that enter surf breaks and harass people,' Bill Hamilton told local newspaper *The Garden Island*. 'I've been here the last 35 years and have only fished for three sharks: one in 1978, the second about eight years ago. [But] we heard continuous stories [of] a big, dangerous animal. There's too many young kids, too many people in the water. I don't think we can accept a second tragedy.'

The fishermen gutted the shark but found no evidence of Bethany's arm or the watch she was wearing. However, the shark's jaws were a perfect fit for the crescent-shaped chunk missing from her surfboard. They then gave the shark's skin to local Hawaiian *kahuna* (priest) Boy Akana to make a ceremonial *pahu pai* drum to 'calm the seas' and local tensions. In stark contrast with Vic Hislop's guilt-free shark hunts, Young told *The Garden Island* he felt 'remorse' for 'taking such a beautiful creature': 'I feel bad about taking the shark, but not as bad as I'd feel if someone [else] had been bit.'

Tiger sharks are considered a 'near threatened' species world-wide due to overfishing (predominantly for fins, not flesh). However, marine biologist Carl Meyer and his University of Hawaii colleagues found that tiger sharks had 'low dietary over-lap' with other species of sharks in Hawaiian waters, so had little competition for food and consequently were common, wide-spread and wide-ranging. This was despite previous efforts by the State of Hawaii to control shark numbers.

After 15-year-old Billy Weaver was attacked and killed by a tiger shark on 13 December 1958, the State of Hawaii culled 4668 sharks from 1959 to 1976, including 554 tiger sharks. However, scientists at the University of Hawaii found that, aside from a small dip in the number of tiger sharks caught from 1967 to 1969, there was no significant decrease in the number of sharks or the rate of shark attacks.

'There were two broad lines of evidence that this shark control stuff was worthless,' Meyer told *Outside* magazine. 'One was critical tracking data showing that these sharks were much more mobile than people believed.' University of Hawaii data showed tiger sharks travelling between islands for distances of up to 318 kilometres a day.

The second was that people were still getting bitten at sites from which many tiger sharks had already been removed by control fishing. So there's just no evidence that shark culling makes the water safer. It's just not demonstrably effective.

Despite the scientific evidence, shark culls have continued to be used as a political response to fatal shark attacks, most recently in Western Australia and Réunion.

'It saddens me to see that,' Mike said. 'From a scientific point of view it's the wrong thing to do. It is a total knee-jerk reaction.'

When 21-year-old Kyle Burden lost his life to a shark while bodyboarding in Western Australia on 4 September 2011, Mike visited Kyle's girlfriend's Facebook page.

'As much as I'm against culling, I saw her sadness and felt like: "Who am I to say this stuff?" It's a really touchy thing when there's lives being lost and people are doing things based on emotion and anger and hate. But when you step back from it all and look at it through a sober lens, it is really not the correct way to mitigate a problem. I'm a strong advocate that coexistence is the way to go and you are not coexisting with anything if you are killing it.'

Coexistence is the catchphrase on Kauai: coexistence between indigenous Hawaiians and *haoles* (white people of European ancestry), between local residents and the 1.2 million tourists who visit the island each year, and between civilisation and nature, including aggressive and dangerous tiger sharks. Mike and Bethany are local heroes and walking warning signs. Like Bite Club in Australia, they use their shared experience to support each other.

'She's like my sister,' Mike said. 'We have this kind of unspoken bond that we're in this club together that nobody else is a part of. It really blows people away when we surf together because we surf together quite a bit. We often have people lined up on the beach watching us – a girl with one arm and a guy with a prosthetic leg riding waves together. It's pretty crazy.'

Mike does not believe there is a silver bullet to stop shark attacks. Yet. He is buoyed by the ongoing development of personal safety devices like the Shark Shield, an electrical shark deterrent tested by the University of Western Australia and the KwaZulu-Natal Sharks Board.

'I don't know enough about these devices to have an opinion, but I do know that if someone were to figure out a fail-proof system, that is a billion-dollar idea,' he said.

'I don't think there is a straightforward answer to how we coexist. I think it's a combination of everything as long as you are not killing. Right now, with the science we have available to us, we don't have a way of protecting people from sharks and shark attacks, but we can use what we do know. I like the approach in Réunion Island, with the divers looking for signs of sharks, for other alerts like helicopters and drones, lifeguards with whistles and horns, nets that are safe … Hopefully, as we learn more about sharks through tracking and satellite tagging, we can find a complete solution that is really effective in letting people enjoy ocean activities and the sharks can keep going on doing their business without being killed.'

Mike has cage dived with great white sharks in New Zealand and does not subscribe to theories about rogue sharks, unbalanced food chains or bloodthirsty, man-eating monsters from *Jaws*.

'When you are below the surface and you have that connection and eye contact it's completely different. It's not scary. It's just beautiful.'

EPILOGUE

THE OCEAN WAS ugly. It was grey and choppy, and a cold wind had been blowing for weeks. Darren Rogers sat in his car, as stony-faced as an Easter Island statue, checking the surf at Shelly Beach like a bad habit.

Darren couldn't remember the last time he'd actually gone surfing here. He'd spent April in Bali, surfing every day, but as winter blossomed into spring, the memory of it faded like a distant dream.

The New South Wales government's $16 million shark management strategy hadn't helped Darren's state of mind. Plans to install an eco-friendly shark net across North Wall to Lighthouse Beach had been scrapped due to ongoing rough seas. The Department of Primary Industries (DPI) had tagged 37 great white sharks off the north coast of NSW during 2015. The sharks' acoustic transmitters were detected whenever they came within 500 metres of satellite-linked listening stations positioned along the coast, from Tweed Heads on the Queensland border to

Forster, some 500 kilometres further south. Darren had installed the SharkSmart app on his phone, which automatically notified him of each satellite transmission.

'It's pinging all the time,' he said.

It's just constant. And that's just the tagged ones. There are lots of whites around close to shore. They are absolutely everywhere. It has definitely made it harder for me.

The ones that freak me out the most are the ones that ping at midnight or at one am or at three am. I just think: 'Fucking hell, they never sleep, they never go away.'

Despite the ongoing shark sightings and seemingly endless stream of satellite transmissions, the mood in Ballina in early spring 2016 was one of cautious optimism. Tourist operators had been buoyed by a stronger than usual summer holiday season, while surfers had enjoyed a memorable winter of waves. There hadn't been a single shark attack recorded on the northern New South Wales coast since Sam Morgan was bitten at North Wall on 10 November 2015. There had been one close encounter – a shark 'as big as a car' knocked 18-year-old Harry Lake off his surfboard at Sharpes Beach, midway between Ballina and Lennox Head, on 26 July 2016. Then, just after 8am on Monday 26 September 2016, the first day of school holidays, a four-metre great white shark mauled 17-year-old local surfer Cooper Allen at North Wall. The attack occurred only a few hundred metres south and in eerily similar conditions to Tadashi Nakahara's fatal encounter in February 2015.

'It was a beautiful day,' Cooper told Channel 7's *Sunday Night* program. 'It was just sunny – it seemed like the perfect day.'

I had literally just paddled out. I was sitting on my board for maybe a second and then 'bang'. Everything is just going through your head. I just remember thinking, 'Am I going to bleed to death? Am I going to die?'

Cooper got lucky. The shark's sharp serrated teeth left four deep puncture wounds on his outer thigh, but narrowly missed the descending branch of the lateral femoral circumflex artery. The teenager, who lives across the road from the beach, told rescuers to 'call an ambulance … but don't tell my Mum'.

Within a few hours, the SharkSmart Twitter account tweeted aerial images of lifeguards on jet-skis shepherding a large great white shark out to sea. The media feeding frenzy followed in hot pursuit. Former Australian prime minister Tony Abbott told Melbourne's 3AW radio station that he couldn't understand 'for the life of me' why shark nets hadn't been installed on the north coast of New South Wales and urged commercial fishermen to cull sharks.

'I don't know why we don't have a commercial shark fishery up there because, frankly, if it's a choice between people and animals, I'm on the side of the people every time,' Abbott said.

Le-Ba Boardriders Club president Don Munro said the latest attack had hardened local attitudes to the NSW government's 'soft' shark mitigation strategy.

'It just reignited that whole fear, frustration, anger about the whole situation,' Don said. 'It's like they're playing Russian roulette with our lives.'

Human life is far more important than animal life. They stopped culling great whites nearly 20 years ago. What we are seeing now is those juveniles fully grown and on the march up the east coast (of Australia).

The sharks were on the march and surfers were on the menu. Sixteen days after Cooper's attack, on October 12, Brunswick Heads surfer Seneca Rus was launched into the air and bitten on the leg at Sharpes Beach. Two weeks later, on October 24, Byron Bay surfer Jade Fitzpatrick was bitten on the thigh by a three-metre great white shark at nearby Broken Head. Then, on the very last day of spring, a four-metre great white shark attacked veteran 62-year-old surfer Colin Rowland at Booti Booti Headland near Forster, south of Ballina; biting his arm, shredding his foot and taking a huge chunk out of his surfboard. It was little wonder that Darren Rogers found it difficult to get back in the water.

The effects are still lingering and I feel guilty that I'm still struggling with it. But it won't win. I'm giving myself some grace. I still love surfing but I'm giving myself some time to just let it happen and not push it. I saw these pictures on Facebook the other day, of a great white shark with its mouth open, and it freaked me out badly because I knew that's what came up and took Tadashi's legs. It's like a virus. It feeds on itself.

The New South Wales government's response to the attacks was to deploy SMART (Shark-Management-Alert-in-Real-Time) drumlines off the coast from where each incident occurred.

The SMART drumlines, which had first been trialled on the north coast in December 2015, are baited hooks linked to satellite communications units, positioned approximately 500 metres offshore and kept afloat by two buoys. When a shark is hooked, the pressure on the line triggers the communications unit, which alerts DPI scientists and contracted fishermen. Within half an hour, the fishermen haul the shark in, the scientists tag it, then it is towed at least one kilometre out to sea and released. The drumlines are set every morning and retrieved every evening.

SMART drumlines were first deployed on Réunion Island in January 2014. They were the brainchild of marine biologist David Guyomard, project manager of Réunion's Regional Fisheries Committee.

'I had the idea after reading about ancient swordfish fishing techniques in Cuba,' Guyomard told *Ocean 71* magazine.

At night, they used to put a burning torch on the buoy over their fishing lines. When a fish took the bait, the flame would fall in the water and from the beach the fishermen were alerted that something was going on.

Guyomard and Réunion shark fisherman Christophe 'Criquet' Perry simply added modern technology, replacing the burning torch with a solar-powered GPS device to alert fishermen when a fish is hooked. If the fish is a large bull shark (1.5 metres and longer) or a large tiger shark (2.5 metres and longer), it is killed, its stomach contents are analysed, its flesh is examined for ciguatoxins and its jaws are kept to help identify the species and size of shark when someone is bitten. If it is any other species of fish it is measured and released. Guyomard told the ABC that the SMART drumlines had been specifically developed 'to minimise the impact on by-catch species and maximise their survival rate by allowing fishermen to go as soon as possible to the (drum-lines) to release the animal caught on the hook'. He suggested that fish hooked by the SMART drumlines were still alive when the fishermen arrive 86% of the time.

'We only aim for the large predators that threaten the population in areas popular for marine activities,' he explained.

We use a specific type of bait and hook, which naturally select the animals that are caught. It's not like the nets used around the world that blindly catch everything, such as turtles and dolphins.

However, the SMART drumline program on Réunion is still controversial. 178 sharks were killed (83 bull sharks and 95 tiger sharks) in the four-year period between August 2012 and August 2016, when culling was conducted intermittently on the island. French oceanographer, professional diver and conservationist François Sarano said the culling of sharks on Réunion was 'plainly unbelievable'.

'[I] strongly believe that the elimination of these predators is not the solution to resolve the crisis and prevent further accidents,' Sarano stated. 'What we should be doing is working towards a balanced ecosystem, which is what the Marine Reserve (on Réunion Island's west coast) is here for.'

A scientific advisor to the legendary Jacques Costeau, Sarano also believes the baited hooks are actually 'attracting large sharks straight into the popular bathing and surfing areas'. While Guyomard has dismissed the theory as a 'myth' without any supporting evidence, it has been backed by high-profile environmental activist Captain Paul Watson. In fact, the Sea Shepherd founder has taken it even further. On a Facebook post, Watson suggested that the drumlines might have contributed to the horrific death of 13-year-old Réunion Island surfer Elio 'Titi' Canestri in April 2015.

'Despite the ban on surfing, the boy and some of his comrades decided to surf; perhaps confident because of the installation, a few hundred meters away, of a drumline 12 days before.'

Scientists from the Marine Reserve Science Council, despite enormous state pressure, despite the constant threats and insults, unanimously said that it was dangerous to bait near surfers and [that] drumlines should not be installed in the reserve and near the beaches.

This entire situation [on Réunion Island] has been created by human activity in over-fishing, elimination of reef sharks, pollution, dumping of sewage, fish guts and animal offal, and compounded by regular heavy rains. It has already been proven that culling does not work but instead contributes to more occurrences.

There have been six fatal shark attacks in the six years since the Mayor of Saint-Leu authorised the culling of sharks on Réunion in August 2012 – twice as many as in the six years prior. One of the few remaining professional fisherman on the island, Thierry Gazzo, accused Réunion's Regional Fisheries Committee of 'disturbing the marine balance with their drumlines in front of popular beaches'. Gazzo told Ocean 71 magazine that bull sharks spend 95% of the their time at a depth of 50 metres or more, while tiger sharks were usually found at least six kilometres offshore. He said that the SMART drumlines were attracting sharks closer to the coast. Like many islanders, Gazzo is not against culling sharks, but suggested a more direct and aggressive approach was required.

> Today, the fishing efforts do not cover the reproduction rates. As long as we decide to cull the bull sharks, we need to do it smartly and get more fish out of the water than what is born, which is far from being the case at the moment.

The SMART drumlines deployed off the New South Wales coast are not designed to kill sharks. Dr Vic Peddemors is chief shark scientist at the NSW Department of Primary Industries (DPI), which co-ordinates the New South Wales government's $16 million shark management strategy. A straight-talking, lantern-jawed South African who has studied sharks for over 30 years, Peddemors said the SMART drumlines deployed in NSW were primarily to mitigate shark attacks.

'Intercepting and catching target sharks (white, tiger and bull sharks) as they travel along our coastline reduces the chances of an interaction with surfers and swimmers,' he explained. 'This is because the captured shark is released offshore. The data indicates that they move away and offshore from the area of capture, effectively reducing potential encounters with people in nearshore waters.'

The released sharks are tagged to help scientists better understand their movements, but also so they can be detected whenever they come within 500 metres of the satellite-linked listening stations positioned along the NSW coast.

'This information assists water users to determine potential risk before they enter the water.'

The monitoring of the movements of tagged sharks is also helping us understand the factors affecting their distribution in coastal waters, so we may one day identify potential environmental conditions correlated with increased risk to surfers and swimmers.

However, this appears a long way away. Peddemors has lamented that the best way to describe the movement of great white sharks is 'like if you drop a bag of marbles'.

'They go everywhere,' he told Triple J radio's *Hack* program. 'That's very frustrating for us because the aim of our research is to try to understand their movements so that we can assist local authorities and the local community in reducing the chances of being bitten.'

While the research will take years, the SMART drumlines have already been hailed as a resounding success by a NSW government under pressure 'to do something'. After the initial trial in 2015, up to 35 SMART drumlines have been deployed daily (weather and ocean conditions permitting) off the coast of Lennox Head, Ballina and Evans Head – a 52-kilometre stretch of ocean that has overtaken Western Australia as the shark attack capital of Australia. A further 10 drumlines have been deployed at other locations along the NSW coast as far south as Ulladulla, almost 1,000 kilometres south of Ballina. 179 sharks were caught by the SMART drumlines over the 10-month period from December 2016 to the end of September 2017. 149 of these were target species (white, tiger and bull sharks), including an astonishing 141 great white sharks, while 98.8% of all sharks hooked were alive when fishermen arrived.

'You can't argue with the data,' NSW Minister for Primary Industries Niall Blair proclaimed. 'SMART drumlines have proven to be five times more effective than mesh nets. We are leading the world in this technology. They protect human life while minimising the impact on marine species.'

After the failed attempt to install eco-barriers at Ballina and Lennox Head, SMART drumlines have become the centrepiece of the NSW government's response to the rising number of shark attacks off its beaches, with the program being expanded up and down the coast. More than 100 drumlines are expected to be in operation in New South Wales by early 2018, supported by aerial surveillance from NSW Surf Life Saving 'Little Ripper' drones.

'No single effective shark bite mitigation approach will be suitable for all of the NSW coastline,' Peddemors warned. 'The coastline is large (2,137 kilometres in length) with many of the most popular surfing spots well away from Surf (Life Saving) Clubs or human habitation.'

A pioneer on the use of technological advances in his research, Peddemors studied the effect of magnets and electropositive metals on Galapagos sharks and is an advocate of personal safety devices like the Shark Shield, which has been independently tested by scientists in Western Australia and South Africa.

I really firmly believe that electric shark repellants work and people should have them on their surfboards. Stop asking the government, stop asking the council, stop asking everyone else to look after your own safety. Look after it yourself.

The New South Wales DPI's SMART drumline data seems to confirm anecdotal evidence of a boom in the number of great white sharks on Australia's east coast, with 37 great whites hooked in the month of September 2017 and 141 over the course of 10 months. Previous studies have estimated an adult population of between 750 and 1200 adult great white sharks on the eastern seaboard, but that number now seems like a radical low-ball.

'It's not that easy to count sharks,' Peddemors told *Hack*. 'The only way to do it is using genetic tools.'

Scientists from Australia's Commonwealth Scientific and Industrial Research Organisation (CSIRO) have been using a range of tools to conduct a long-awaited population study of great white sharks, including tagging (incorporating NSW DPI data), aerial surveys and close-kin genetics, which has been used to estimate wildlife populations for animals like the Antarctic blue whale. The great white shark is responsible for the most unprovoked shark attacks (314) and most fatal shark attacks (80) worldwide, according to International Shark Attack File (ISAF) data (1580-2016). In Australian waters, the great white shark has been a protected species since 1999. That may soon change, with the Australian government foreshadowing changes to the Environment Protection and Biodiversity Conservation Act if the CSIRO study finds the great white is no longer endangered.

'Every fisherman knows the numbers are exploding,' former prime minister Tony Abbott told *The Australian* newspaper. 'They are not an endangered species.'

Across the Pacific, the arrival of spring on the California coast coincided with an unprecedented surge in shark activity. It began on 18 March 2017, when a 5-metre great white shark launched kayaker Brian Correiar into the air just behind the breakwater at

Cannery Row in Monterey Bay on the central California coast. Shaky phone footage of the shark repeatedly attacking Correiar's sea kayak went viral on YouTube. In a blog post, Correiar described the shark using the 14-foot kayak 'as a chew toy' and said that he was 'really nervous' that he would be next.

'It was like a horror movie,' he wrote. 'The shark came toward me, dropped the kayak, then dove straight down below me where I couldn't see it. I was sure I was done.'

Fortunately, a passing sailboat plucked Correiar from the water, but the incident set off a frenzy of shark sightings and beach closures along the California coast. On April 29, a 3-metre great white shark attacked Leeanne Ericson as she waded in shallow water at San Onofre Beach near San Clemente, south of Los Angeles. The mother of three lost half of her right leg in the attack and spent more than a month in hospital, fighting for her life. On May 21, San Clemente beaches were closed again when more than two dozen sharks were spotted loitering close to shore, while record shark sightings were logged at nearby Capistrano Beach from May to July.

The great white shark has been a protected species in Californian waters since 1994. California State University shark expert Dr Chris Lowe said a rebounding shark population meant that more encounters were 'the new reality'.

'The number of seals, sea lions and otters that have been observed with white shark bites have been steadily increasing since 2002,' Dr Lowe told the *San Francisco Chronicle*.

> Shark populations are coming back, so obviously encounters will increase. And we need those sharks. They're really important in keeping our oceans healthy. People are going to have to learn to share the waves.

Dr Lowe speculated that warmer waters caused by El Niño and global climate change had made southern California beaches a 'more favourable' nursery for juvenile great whites. Similarly, almost all of the 141 great white sharks hooked by SMART drumlines off the New South Wales coast have been sub-adults, 2 to 3 metres in length – the largest was a 3.6-metre female great white caught off Tuncurry Beach on 16 September 2017, half the size of the 6.2-metre 'world record' shark Vic Hislop caught near Phillip Island in 1987.

'We believe that the reason sharks bite humans [is related to the fact] that all of these bites tend to be [from] sharks in the less than 3-metre range,' Vic Peddemors told *Hack*.

> Between 2–3 metres, they tend to change their diet from eating solely fish to eating fish and marine mammals. At that stage they realise they need something more, something bigger, to sustain themselves. The only way they can test something to see if it's edible is to bite it.

The impact of these exploratory bites is devastating.

There is a shrine in the Nakahara family home in Japan. Alongside a statue of Buddha, candles, a singing bowl and incense burners are mementoes of Tadashi, including a shiny, speckled cowrie shell from Shelly Beach.

'The cowrie is my favourite shell,' Darren Rogers explained.

> They are very rare and I found it on the beach the week before [the attack]. I gave it to Tadashi's family when they came out from Japan. I rehearsed a speech and read it out

in Japanese. I learnt how to bow properly and then I gave them the cowrie shell. It was tremendously important to me.

From the car park at Ballina Head, Darren can see the length of coast from Black Head and Shelly Beach to Lighthouse Beach and North Wall. In 2015, there were five shark attacks along this 3.5-kilometre strip of sand, including the fatal attack on Tadashi Nakahara. In 2016, Cooper Allen was mauled by a great white shark just metres from shore.

'I used to drive to this spot every single day,' Darren said.

Every day. Obsessively. No matter what, I had to come. It sounds funny, but just to check that everything was all right. The mouth of that river is the most dangerous spot on the coast because of the bull sharks and the great whites coming around the corner, heading up and down the coast. In my opinion, it's only a matter of time until someone else gets bitten.

It will happen again. And there's nothing that can stop it.

Brooke Mason finished her afternoon shift at the Royal Hobart Hospital. Now in her third year studying Medicine at the University of Tasmania, Brooke's cheeks were flushed as she walked up Campbell Street to her car, carrying cupcakes she'd bought at a cake stall. She'd prefer not to talk about sharks, but she does anyway, somewhat reluctantly.

'It's always on your mind,' she confessed.

But I've actually been a lot better with surfing the last few months. The surf has been kind of pumping and because it's been so good lately, I've realised how much I love it and how much it makes me happy. I'm in a much better place.

Small things have helped. Brooke discussed the incident with a psychiatrist who had served in Afghanistan and is an expert in post-traumatic stress disorder. She spoke on the phone to Dave Pearson from Bite Club. She watched Mick Fanning's triumphant return to Jeffreys Bay and was inspired to take a surf trip to the Gold Coast. She also started speaking in schools about positive body image as part of the Fresh Faced Friday campaign.

'Since the shark attack, I'm more passionate about talking to young people, especially young girls,' she said.

Before I started speaking in schools I thought: 'How am I going to do this?' So, I just told them about my own life. I talked to the kids about how the rough things in life make you resilient. I've had a pretty simple life compared to so many people, but I saw a guy get attacked by a shark. After that, the things that I worried about felt so insignificant. It made me realise that life is precious and terrifying things happen every day. You have to do the things you love.

Life is precious. Terrifying things do happen every day.

On 20 January 2017, my wife and I were walking up Bourke Street towards the Melbourne CBD. It was a rare trip into the city without children. We planned to have lunch at a Vietnamese restaurant on Swanston Street. My wife wanted to see an exhibition at the National Gallery of Victoria while I had a work meeting later in the afternoon. There was a huddle of people at the William Street intersection, so we rode the lights and crossed over to the southern side of the street. As we crossed Queen Street, a car came hurtling towards us on the footpath, skittling pedestrians as it sped under the scaffolding overhanging the corner of Bourke and Queen. Time slowed, 'like flashes in a film'. A man in a camouflage rain jacket bounced across the bonnet. The driver didn't flinch. He was unshaven with dead eyes and an unlit cigarette dangling from his mouth. I grabbed my wife with both hands and pushed her towards the curb. I felt the car suck the air from around us. A body cartwheeled through the air and landed in the middle of the street. I held my wife as gunshots echoed off the high-rise office buildings, heavily armoured police surrounded the intersection and office workers applied CPR. But the crumpled body did not move. The angle of its limbs was all wrong.

'He's dead,' I said quietly as I ushered my wife across the street, down Hardware Lane and away from the scene.

The man was one of six people killed in the Bourke Street tragedy. He had just finished lunch with his wife and they were walking back to work together when he was struck as he crossed Queen Street. Their daughter was barely 18 months old.

Among the innocent victims of Bourke Street were a 3-month-old baby and a 10-year-old girl. Another 30 people were seriously injured.

Shell-shocked, my wife and I went to the gallery. We took the train back to Geelong and made a statement at the Geelong Police Station. We undertook trauma counselling. I stayed up late, binge-watching *Game of Thrones*. I drank too much. My small world felt like it had fractured and I fumbled to make sense of something so senseless. I grasped for meaning, for some higher purpose, obscured by emotion. Eventually, I decided to go surfing, where the ocean was my confidant.

For the past 30 years, surfing has been my beautiful addiction. But when I needed it most, the ocean along Victoria's Surf Coast was empty, stung by a rush of shark sightings and beach closures. I spent early mornings in the car park of my local surf spot with the dawn patrol – a handful of hardcore devotees, hard-wired by habit. The swell was small and clean, fanned by a gentle offshore wind, with an occasional lefthander reeling towards the shore. But there was no rush for the wetsuits and wax. Instead there was nervous chatter about bronze whalers and baitfish. The local builder said he'd spotted a dorsal fin slicing through the shorebreak while walking his dog at nearby Fairhaven Beach, which had been closed five times since Christmas, spooking the summer holidaymakers. Meanwhile, 18 people had drowned in New South Wales in the space of 10 days, between Christmas Day 2016 and 3 January 2017. The ocean seemed no place to seek solace.

But I went surfing. And I haven't stopped. I surfed nearby Cathedral Rock a few weeks after Marcel Brundler was bitten by a 4-metre great white while surfing there on 30 August 2017 in what was the most serious shark attack on Victoria's west coast in recent memory. Kelly Slater once said: 'If you're afraid of sharks, stay out of the ocean'. I would be lying if I said that I wasn't afraid of sharks. They are regularly swimming somewhere in the back of my mind in the pre-dawn darkness as I splash around the shallows trying to catch a wave before work, daycare drop-off or Sunday morning swimming lessons. But knowledge is power. I know that life is short and I know that you have to do the things you love.

REFERENCES

Field Book of Giant Fishes, John Norman and Francis Fraser, Putnam, 1949

Great White Shark: Myth and reality, Alexandrine Civard-Racinais, Firefly Books, 2012

Jaws, Peter Benchley, Doubleday, 1974

Natural History of the Fishes of Massachusetts: Embracing a practical essay on angling, Jerome Van Croninsfield Smith, Allen and Ticknor, 1833

Shark: Fear and beauty, Jean-Marie Ghislain, Thames & Hudson, 2014

Shark!: Killer tales from the dangerous depths, Robert Reid, Allen & Unwin, 2010

Shark Attack, Victor Coppleson, Angus and Robertson, 1958

Sharks, edited by John D. Stevens, Checkmark Books, 1999

Soul Surfer: A true story of faith, family, and fighting to get back on the board, Bethany Hamilton and Rick Bundschuh with Sheryl Berk, MTV Books, 2004

Surf for Your Life, Tim Baker and Mick Fanning, Ebury Australia, 2010

Surfing's Greatest Misadventures: Dropping in on the unexpected, edited by Paul Diamond, Wilderness Press, 2006

The Book of Sharks, Richard Ellis, Knopf, 1989

The Devil's Teeth: A true story of obsession and survival among America's great white sharks, Susan Casey, Macmillan, 2005

The Encyclopedia of Surfing, Matt Warshaw, Mariner Books, 2005

The Expression of the Emotions in Man and Animals, Charles Darwin, John Murray, 1872

The Mammoth Book of Shark Attacks, Alex MacCormick, Robinson, 2013

The Natural History of Sharks, Thomas Lineaweaver and Richard Backus, Deutsch, 1970

The Shark: Splendid savage of the sea, Jacques-Yves Cousteau, Cassell, 1974

Vic Hislop Shark Man, Vic Hislop, Vic Hislop, 1993

ACKNOWLEDGEMENTS

THIS BOOK WOULD never have happened without the love and support of my wife, Karen, and two boys, Felix and Theodore. I also leaned heavily on my parents, Pat and Jenny McAloon, and incredibly supportive in-laws, Easton and Celia James, whilst being urged on by family, friends and colleagues, particularly Drew Ryan and Katie Rafferty. I owe an ongoing debt of gratitude to those who sank in deep water so I could swim, particularly Damien McAloon, Julia Reeves, Pat and Jenny, Drew and Shaz, the Foster family, Jak Dyer and Jon Frank. I would also like to acknowledge the generous guidance of Anyez Lindop and Rose Michael, who helped me keep the faith when it was in short supply, and to give a shout out to the staff at Geelong Regional Libraries, Geelong Grammar School's Fisher Library and the State Library of Victoria. Respect.

My very special thanks to Fran Berry at Hardie Grant, who diverted my navel gazing, and my fabulous and fabulously patient editors, Meelee Soorkia, Allison Hiew and Anna Collett. Thank you.

This book was inspired by the generous and courageous contributions of Darren Rogers, Brooke Mason, Mick Fanning, Dave Pearson and Mike Coots. Yours is the Earth and everything that's in it.

It was written in memory of Tadashi Nakahara. A surfer. There, but for the grace of God, go I.